SAVAGE
PARK

ALSO BY AMY FUSSELMAN

The Pharmacist's Mate

8

A MEDITATION
ON PLAY, SPACE, *and* RISK *for*
AMERICANS WHO ARE
NERVOUS, DISTRACTED, *and*
AFRAID TO DIE

SAVAGE
PARK

Amy Fusselman

HOUGHTON MIFFLIN HARCOURT
Boston   New York
2015

For information about permission to reproduce
selections from this book, write to Permissions,
Houghton Mifflin Harcourt Publishing Company,
215 Park Avenue South, New York, New York 10003.

www.hmhco.com

Library of Congress Cataloging-in-Publication Data
Fusselman, Amy.
Savage park : a meditation on play, space, and risk for Americans
who are nervous, distracted, and afraid to die / Amy Fusselman.
    pages cm
ISBN 978-0-544-30300-3 (hardback) – ISBN 978-0-544-57020-7 (trade paper) –
ISBN 978-0-544-30329-4 (ebook)
1. Fusselman, Amy. 2. Authors, American – 21st century – Biography.
3. Playgrounds – Japan – Tokyo. 4. Play (Philosophy)
5. Space – Philosophy. 6. Risk-taking (Psychology). I. Title.
PS3606.U86Z46 2015
813.6 – dc23
[B]

Book design by Greta D. Sibley

Printed in the United States of America
DOC 10 9 8 7 6 5 4 3 2 1

All photos courtesy of the author unless otherwise noted.

Part opener illustrations by Patrick Barry

Parts of this book have appeared in different forms
in *The Rumpus, Two Serious Ladies,* and
the *Columbia Journal.*

To the players in playgrounds everywhere

CONTENTS

PART I

PART II

PART I

1

NSEW

| 1 |

Early one spring morning several years ago, I received an e-mail from my USSR-born, New York City–bred theater-director friend Yelena inviting me and my family (which then consisted of my husband, Frank, and our two sons, King and Mick, ages five and two) to visit her and her family (which then consisted of her husband, R, and their two sons, Chuck and Gen, ages four and one) at their new home in Tokyo, with the understanding that if we chose to come, we would stay for at least a month.

I do not believe the English language contains a word that expresses all that this gesture was. Her invitation to us was a feat. She inhabited her space with such generosity that she enlarged it. And then, from that expanse, she called to us: Come in.

She summoned us without much consideration, it seemed, for the space between us. The distance between New York City and Tokyo, after all, is almost seven thousand miles. It was as if she didn't view the journey we would have to take to get to her as daunting, formidable, or even, really, interesting.

The distance was just space, for her. And she did not see space as an enemy. She was not worried, as I was, about what it would be like to fly thirteen hours with small children, never having flown longer than two and a half hours with them before. She did not regard space as a thing to be crossed in a belabored, linear way, like Columbus suffering for months, sick and arthritic, in his leaky, worm-rotted ship as it bobbed unevenly toward an unknown continent.

Space, for her, was like a toy. It was a thing that could and should be manipulated; a medium to be expanded, contracted, and fiddled with. As far as she was concerned, we would get on a plane, which was not a machine for crossing space but a machine for contracting time, and we would be here/there in the blink of an eye.

When we got the invitation, my husband, Frank, and I looked at each other: When would we ever have an opportunity like this again?

Frank and I told the boys we were going on a journey to Japan. I pointed out New York on the globe. "From here," I said, dragging my finger across the world as I simultaneously spun it, "to there," I said.

They glanced at us, unfazed, and continued pushing their

smiling toy trains around the figure eight of wooden track that was set up on the train table.

| 2 |

Nervous about the long flight from NYC to Tokyo, I decided that we would fly from NYC to LA first and then stay over there for a night in order to cut down on the number of hours per flight and get used to the time change.

Of course, this only made the whole transition worse – more drawn out, and thus more nerve-racking – but I had not yet wrapped my brain around the concept that traveling across space was not a thing to be suffered through.

Naturally, the journey was long and arduous. After arriving in LA, we dropped our luggage at a hotel, visited a train museum called Travel Town, returned to the hotel and slept, fitfully, and then woke up groggy the next morning, only to pack our bags and head to the airport again. Then we flew.

When we finally loaded our sweaty, sleepy selves into a cab outside the Tokyo airport, I dropped my head back on the pristine white doily placed like a pressed flower on the top of the seatback and slept like a drooling drunk, if drooling drunks can still be nervous. I was nervous in particular because I wasn't sure if we had accurately communicated our destination to the driver; he spoke no English, and we spoke no Japanese. With no idea where we were or where we were going, we couldn't even tell if we were lost.

I rode like this, almost unconscious, my head flung back, my mouth open, my eyes half closed, passing indecipherable signs in the dark. When we pulled up in front of Yelena's apartment – how long did it take to get there? A minute? An hour? – she was sitting on her stoop in a witch's hat. It was Halloween. Her four-year-old son, Chuck, who was dressed as a skeleton, stood beside her holding a bowl of candy.

I hugged Yelena. "Trick or treat," I said.

Frank and I shouldered our heavy bags and our sack-like, sleeping children and carried them up the steps and into Yelena's apartment, the chocolate Chuck had just given us melting in our mouths. I set Mick down on one of the two foldout couches that were to be our beds for the next three weeks and then lay down beside him. Yelena tried to convince me to stay awake – it was about six in the evening – but I could not.

Sure enough, at three in the morning, Mick and I were up. We snuck out of the apartment in order not to wake anyone, and I put him in his stroller and strolled him through the dark, silent streets, talking nonsense – it was the Day of the Dead, I remember informing him helpfully – trying and failing to find the logic of Manhattan's crude but reliable grid in Tokyo's delicately unfolding swirl.

We ended up sitting in the deserted, lit-up parking lot of an all-night convenience store at four thirty in the morning, sharing a chocolate steamed bun. Mick washed it down with some strawberry milk. I drank hot coffee out of a can.

Yelena was right, I understood then, in her dismissal of what it took to get here. What was harder was this other thing she was encouraging me to do, which was to call her home my home and, beyond that, to call wherever I was my home; to view space not as a place that is mine here, and yours there, but as a venue that is ours and that we are in together.

Being exhausted and, I thought, out of my element, I continued to resist her and her big ideas.

| 3 |

Among the first things we learn about space, as infants having very recently arrived in it, is that we can't just leave it. We can move ourselves around in it, and we can be transported in it, but the fact is, we are here.

Years go by. We grow accustomed to this strange and interesting situation – this hereness. And, as adults, what we end up saying to our children about space and our human place in it is mostly a long and complicated narrative of how to move our bodies safely and respectfully in relation to other people and things.

This adult-generated stream of language – which basically completely ignores the idea that space is a medium that can

A place to sit and rest, Hanegi Playpark, Tokyo

be experienced and responded to sensitively – is like a darkly magical incantation, in that it makes space disappear.

What children receive, then, is the notion that space does not exist but people and things do, and it is people and things that must be navigated to, from, and around, and it is people and things that represent hazards or pleasures. They are not told that space itself is a beautiful and powerful medium that we are all connected in and through, and that space can, and should, be felt.

Of course it is understandable that we adults should hold this rather shortsighted perspective. There are many wonderful things to focus on here on earth. The trees are lovely, the food tastes great, there are toys, and, not least important, other human beings are fantastically interesting and may serve as warm, comforting ballast to cling to as we float along, all of us more or less aware of the fundamental situation: that we are here, for reasons unknown, and one day we will not be here, also for reasons unknown.

| 4 |

There was a swimming demonstration at Mick's Upper West Side day camp this morning. It's almost the end of the season, and parents were invited in to see how their children's swimming had improved after the lessons provided by the camp all summer.

The parents gathered in the lobby after drop-off, chatting, with sweaty, clear plastic cups of iced coffee in hand. At 9:00 sharp we were led into the pool area, where we were instructed to walk single file halfway around the pool and then sit on a narrow metal bench bolted to the wall. The children were then led in, in their swimsuits and goggles, to sit on the metal bleachers directly across the pool from us.

With everyone in place, the show began. Clutching her clipboard, the aquatics director introduced herself and then launched into an explanation of how the children were supervised in the pool.

There were eight plastic orange chairs stationed around the pool, she explained. In each of these chairs, a lifeguard sat and watched a group of six to eight children as they worked with another lifeguard in the water. There were never fewer than two lifeguards – one watching, one teaching – per group. There were also helpers, people who were not certified as lifeguards – floaters, she called them – who were in the pool during this time, keeping their eyes on the kids.

She turned to the lifeguards, who were standing beside the bleachers: Take your places, she said.

Eight lifeguards trotted over to sit in the orange chairs; eight lowered themselves into the water.

She turned to the floaters, who were also standing beside the bleachers: Go ahead, she said.

Sixteen floaters splashed into the water and fanned out across the pool.

She turned to the children: Go to your groups, she said.

The children filed out of the bleachers and dispersed to the orange chairs, where they sat down at the edge of the pool and churned the water with their feet, the only ones in this humid, chlorine-y aquadome who weren't completely one of two things: in the water, or out.

In order to comply with city safety standards, the aquatics director told us, each child was assigned a buddy.

This camp was well run, all right; that word, *buddy,* was a cue. Upon hearing it, each child grabbed his partner's hand, and each hand-clasped pair of children flung their hand-knot overhead like a flag, and the aquatics director stopped speaking to us and began performing for us, with the following call-and-response:

"Group one?" she called to the lifeguard standing in the water with the group-one children.

"Seven," the group-one lifeguard said, meaning seven children were in the group.

"Group two?" she called to the lifeguard standing in the water with the group-two children.

"Six," the group-two lifeguard said.

And so on, the numbers ping-ponging in the air over the pool, sailing from the aquatics director standing beside the now empty bleachers, her brow tense; to the eight lifeguards standing in the water, smiling as they faced their groups of children; to the eight lifeguards sitting in the orange chairs, watching silently from their colorful posts; to the children themselves sitting at the edge of the pool, their flagpole arms held high, their buddy-ness unfurled, their reliance on and connection to other people absolutely joyful and absolutely grave; to us, smiling across the water at our children, each of us knowing like no one and everyone else here the exact, happy grief of an inviolable responsibility to another person; to the floaters standing in the pool, casually arranged in this humid air, like party balloons scattered on a picnic blanket.

The numbers having been run, the aquatics director stopped singing and told the children to enter the pool.

There was a pause. The children unclasped their hands and lowered them to their laps, birds adroitly returning to their nests.

We sat clutching our empty cups as the children, from their perches, with every adult eye on them, leapt.

| 5 |

In general, in this country, we hold dear several conflicting views of space.

To clarify, the space I am referring to is small-*s* space, or space on earth. This small-*s* space is commonly regarded as being completely different from big-*S* Space, or outer space. That is, whereas big-*S* Space is often seen as a mysterious and powerful thing worthy of constant scrutiny and wildly expensive exploration, small-*s* space frequently just disappears, and no one notices.

It happens like this: You are here; you are driving to the store. You exist and the store exists. You are generally far more aware of the time that it takes – stuck at that red light again, harrumph – to cross the space between your house and the store than you are of the space itself, the space that contains the car, the house, the store, the light, and you.

This is not to say that people do not believe in space. Most of us do believe in the concept of space as the place where things and people are located. Space in this sense is like a giant, invisible handbag, and we are lipsticks and mirrors bouncing around in it. But for the most part, space does not exist for us as a thing we consider ourselves immersed in and connected with. We just do not, in a thousand large and small ways, pay attention to it.

This prejudice is understandable. Small-*s* space has the misfortune of being invisible, and most humans are hugely dependent on, and seduced by, the power of sight. We see through space to people and things; it is people and things that exist for us.

We see through space to things we want – lunch, bed, a lover, the phone. We steer our bodies through the invisibleness to get to what we want. We do not pay much attention to the experience of steering. We look; we mobilize; we arrive. We experience how long the mobilizing takes. What it feels like walking through space, floating across the room to answer the phone – we do not generally experience that with much sensitivity, especially those of us who are healthy and for whom the process of mobilization is easy and causes no pain.

Much of this approach is learned.

| 6 |

The first place Yelena took us, on our first day in Tokyo, was the Shinagawa Aquarium.

The Shinagawa was about par for the course, as aquariums go. What I found most interesting about it was the relief I felt, wandering around, in not understanding what I was hearing. It was not my first trip to a foreign country, but it was my first trip to a foreign country where I knew almost none of the language. Knowing almost no words of a language, I found, was completely different from knowing twenty or thirty words and a few phrases. The few words and phrases kept me listening. Without them, it was as if I were swimming in a different medium, a medium I had previously been unaware of, the medium of human-made sound.

I detached from my old way of listening. And knowing that I was not alone and that I could rely on my husband and friend for communicating any urgent matters, I was free to revel in being released from the burden of constantly hearing words that I could not help but decode, muse upon, or judge. I stopped listening for meaning; that is, I dropped my continual engagement with language as an omnipresent, aural mathematics assignment, a one-to-one, sound-equals-word-equals-meaning equation that had to immediately be solved and responded to. I simply let it go.

Instead, I listened to the shades, colors, and tones of language as music, wondering if this freedom I felt, this detachment from the demands of human speech, was a feeling enjoyed by infants. I walked around like this with my family, the music bubbling around me, the impossibly beautiful aquatic creatures floating by me in their transparent boxes, and then I followed Yelena and her sons to sit in the stands and watch the dolphin show.

Two really cute Japanese girls stood on a narrow ledge at the edge of the pool. Both wore the headsets that I associate with customer-service representatives. Their voices were amplified. It goes without saying that I could not understand what they said. It seemed that the dolphins could, though, and the dolphins leapt up impressively, jumping through hoops held high by the girls, and then they tasted some fish.

Disconnected from the show's narrative, I watched what then became a very elaborate way of being fed: the dolphins mastered their bodies in space, exhibiting their tricks and their leaps, in order to receive food from the headsetted young women. The small gesture that the audience was not even supposed to notice – the feeding – became the main event once I was freed from listening to the girls' patter and having it organize what I was seeing.

| 7 |

One of several places where many of us do acknowledge that we are experiencing space is at a restaurant. At restaurants, we eat, drink, and take in the space or, more specifically, a quality of the space, which we call its atmosphere.

The kind of atmosphere one might experience at a restaurant and how, exactly, one goes about feeling it are not subjects that are generally discussed at length in polite company or studied in depth in high school. Instead, each of us approaches a restaurant with expectations and attitudes accumulated through a convoluted personal osmosis that varies wildly according to one's age, place, and income.

When you enter a restaurant or café, you usually assume the place will be something along the lines of warm, clean, and nice – words one might also use to describe Mommy – and this is not incidental, it seems to me, because there are so few man-made places in the public landscape where people acknowledge that space exists to the extent that they describe it as having an atmosphere at all, so it seems significant that the one place where most of us anticipate feeling a space is also a place where we expect to be fed.

That we should conflate eating with experiencing space makes sense, however, considering that one of a human's first and most enduring experiences of being here is likely being fed at the breast of his or her mother. In your first days, you are fed by, warmed by, sheltered by, and comforted by a who, a who that is actually, in these earliest moments, less of a who and more of a where.

If you're going to be brave enough – and it generally does take some courage – to acknowledge the existence of, and experience your relationship with, space, it is logical that you would want to do that in a place that you designate to be the space equivalent of a mom, a place where you will be warm, secure, and fed.

There is nothing wrong with this construct, of course; *bon appétit.* The only reason I point it out at all is simply that it underscores all the places where this construct does not exist; that is, where an atmosphere is not expected or experienced, which is to say, just about everywhere that isn't a restaurant, hotel lobby, bar, airport lounge, or similar public space.

Yet, of course, atmosphere does exist. It is a quality of space that is present everywhere, all the time, and experiencing it is a free and ongoing privilege of being human and being alive. One does not need to enter a restaurant – one certainly does not need to spend money – to have access to it.

It's as if we already feel that arriving here, in this time/

place, is more or less like being thrown in the pool. We can't, we think, spend too much time dwelling on what the water is like. Instead, our approach is more along the lines of *Hurry up, already! Swim!*

| 8 |

A day or two after the aquarium jaunt, Yelena took us to a playground. The playgrounds are fantastic in Tokyo, she kept telling us.

The first playground she wanted to introduce us to was one she and Chuck called the Junk Playground.

As guests in her house – our stuff was strewn across her compact living room, where the four of us were sleeping on two bright-red-and-yellow foldout couches that we dutifully returned to their upright positions each morning – we respectfully submitted to whatever itinerary she had for us.

Frank and I gathered our backpacks and our children and followed Yelena and her children to the subway, slowly getting our bearings around the loop of the Yamanote line. We negotiated the subway stairs, the subway elevator, the departure platform, the train itself, the arrival platform, more stairs, the sidewalk, the sidewalk some more, the corner with the traffic lights, and finally, at last, we opened the playground gate, where we promptly stopped in our slow, heavy mastodon-family tracks.

To our right was an old steam engine. To our left was a decommissioned bulldozer. I could see a fire truck and a backhoe in the distance; all were hugely, incontestably, still.

The boys took off running.

Frank and I followed, pushing Mick's suddenly very fragile-seeming travel stroller through what amounted to a heavy-machinery graveyard.

The Junk Playground, or Haginaka Park, as it is known, is a lovely place in the Ota Ward of Tokyo. The machines sitting there are dead, yes, but they still reverberate with traces of their former force: a yellow steamroller sitting near the playground entrance, its cab empty above its motionless barrel, has all the mysterious beauty of the Sphinx.

I relaxed on a bench with Frank and Yelena and ate delicious sushi from a convenience store as my boys scampered gleefully over objects that had always been off-limits to them.

Eventually, all four boys became very engaged with two boats: one large rowboat and one fishing boat, both partially submerged in concrete. Someone had had the brilliant idea

FRANK L. SNIDER

King rolling tires into the rowboat, Haginaka Park

of surrounding the boats with tires. The boys spent a solid ninety minutes – it would have been longer if we had allowed it – negotiating where and how to roll as many tires as possible into the boats. It was an urgent task, and the graveyard rang with their yelled commands to one another.

Sitting there, drinking coffee – my normally fairly modest coffee consumption jumped about threefold during this trip – I thought how hungry my boys always seemed in their play for moments when their actions could take on real gravity, and how seldom in my parenting of them I took this hunger into consideration. It was as if the things they hungered for were so impossible to satisfy – no, we can't have an airliner for lunch today – that I just had to dismiss their desires completely.

And suddenly I had an image of myself as a fourth-grader on a sunny Saturday afternoon sitting at my dad's desk, hunkered over his manual typewriter, spending hours writing my last will and testament, divvying up my stuffed animals and skating trophies among my family and friends. I must have produced, as an elementary-schooler, at least ten of these wills. I also remembered that my parents cast a rather bemused eye on this project, which annoyed me immensely: I was serious. I was going to die, and I knew it, and I was preparing for it as best I could.

I would have loved for someone to speak to me then, earnestly and without condescension, about death, and what it was, and what we did about it while we were alive. But that was impossible. So I consoled myself with my will-writing activity, and there was nothing funny about it, and the fact that my parents thought I was being cute in these efforts only solidified my disdain for what they considered productive uses of my time.

I emerged from this memory still feeling indignant and took stock of my current situation: far from home, out of my comfort zone, without privacy or refuge, exhausted, grumpy, and uncomfortably beholden to my kinda crazy friend.

I stroked the arm of my foul-weather coat and watched as the boys worked to feed the boat against the clock.

I must have come here for something, I told myself.

| **9** |

Last winter I was waiting for the uptown train at Thirty-Fourth Street. There were two trains that could arrive, the C and the E. I wanted the C, but if the E came, which was the more likely event, I would take it.

The C came after all. I got on it.

I sat there, feeling good, my music on. I had new earbuds: two blue Lego bricks.

I got off at Seventy-Second, which lets you out on Central Park West in front of the Dakota. I love that building. I love the black iron railing as you exit the subway, with the Poseidons and serpents swirling; they're like old men friends walking their dogs.

I walked down Seventy-Second toward Columbus and took the bricks out of my ears.

Windy.

Two young women ran by me. One had her mitten over her mouth. She was shrieking something to her friend in a foreign language.

I heard a weird sound that I thought was perhaps me-chanical.

Windy. Pushing ahead.

I kept going and recognized the sound as a human moan.

I could see, down Seventy-Second, that traffic had been blocked off at Columbus. A crowd had formed in the street, in the shape of an hourglass: the top and bottom of the hour-glass were the sidewalks on either side, and the tiny canal was in the middle of the street, where the man who was the source of the sound was lying on his side next to his twisted bike, clutching his knee.

I walked into the configuration far enough that I was a grain of sand halfway down one side of the glass.

A young man in his twenties was alternating between kneeling next to the injured man, patting him gently, and standing up and whirling around in a long brown coat like a Wild West gunman, only instead of shooting at us, he was looking beseechingly into each person's grain-of-sand-in-an-hourglass face.

After a few whirls back and forth, he finally called out, "Is anyone here a doctor?"

It was a simple yes-or-no question, but it was impossible to answer. It was impossible to think straight with that sound, that excruciatingly painful human sound, which was so small and big simultaneously that it changed the landscape: it made all the gorgeous old buildings on that block – the Dakota, the Majestic, the Franconia, the Hotel Olcott, the Bancroft, the Oliver Cromwell – change so that they were no longer build-ings – that is, human-made structures, ornately decorated by humans outside for humans inside. Instead, they were buildings that did not care about humans, inside or out. They were stones, monolithic and looming, and we who were standing on the street were no longer on the street; we were knee-deep in a cold river flowing at the bottom of a stone canyon. And the painful sound was there, and we were there, and we could not contain the sound, and we could not change it, we just, all of us, stood there, still, with the sound rushing up and around, past us, higher, making the old, solemn stones stand up and then hunch over like perplexed new fathers bending down to look in the crib.

I am not a doctor. I started running down the block, looking for one.

I could see my breath. I ran past the door of the slick pediatric ophthalmologist I had taken both my sons to, to find out that their eyes were fine. I ran past the door of the not-slick adult ophthalmologist I had been to a month before, for the first time ever, to find out that I finally needed reading glasses.

I kept going. I was almost at the subway, with the park in front of me.

I turned around and ran back to the adult ophthalmologist.

The doctor was sitting at the receptionist's desk fiddling on the computer as I burst in the door.

"There's a guy hurt in the street," I said. "Can you help?"

"Did someone call 911?" he asked quickly.

"Yes," I said, thinking, *I bet.*

He came out with me without stopping to put his coat on. Once we were in the cold, he turned to me, his eyes widening: "I hear him," he said.

We ran into the crowd. I took him into the hourglass, then stopped, as before, a few feet before hitting the center; he walked into the center alone. I watched as he stood over the injured man. He stood over him with his legs apart and his hands on his hips. He was a trim man, with his shirt tucked in and his tie fluttering. He was a good ophthalmologist, I thought, somewhat insanely.

I saw him tell the Wild West un-gunman that he was a doctor. The guy looked grateful and stepped aside.

The sound had continued all this time, not really changing too much in pitch or intensity, just an unfathomable human noise filling up the block like the silence of a cathedral. People were behaving as they would in a cathedral's huge space: milling around, heads down, chewing gum, crushing tissues, closing their eyes. Not ecstatic to be there, perhaps, but unable to leave just yet.

About a minute later the ambulance pulled up, and the medics came out. My doctor gestured to the moaning man, and one medic trudged back to the ambulance and got the gurney.

I turned and walked to the sidewalk as the medics hoisted the man onto the gurney and pushed him toward, and then into, the truck.

When I turned back, about ten paces later, I saw my ophthalmologist walking toward me.

"Too bad," he said. "Broken leg."

We talked about my eyes for a minute, and then he left.

The people who formed the hourglass broke up.

I sat on a stoop and collected myself as Seventy-Second returned to its natural state.

A few minutes later I went on my way, twisting the tiny blue bricks back into my ears.

| **10** |

These two very commonly held perspectives of space – that it does not exist, or that it exists as a safe, comforting place with an atmosphere – are almost diametrically opposed. They are like the directions north and south.

The second pair of commonly held perspectives, or east and west, are as follows: first, that space is annoyingly in the way; second, that space is a terrifying black hole into which we will one day disappear.

The idea that space is in the way hardly needs elucidating. Every day, people move through space while experiencing it as an obstacle. As a resident of New York City, I can't count the conversations I have had about the merits of avoiding any type of commute for any reason at all across the length or breadth of the city.

This is not specific to New York, of course. Part of being here in space, with a body, is adjusting to this experience of having to take time – sometimes a lot of time – to make one's way through space.

Finally, space is the place into which we are born; it is where we grow old, have accidents, and die. This is why space is also fundamentally terrifying. We must have a respectful relationship with it – we must learn the crucial principles of how our bodies and space relate – or we will not survive long.

All four of these cardinal perspectives – that space does not exist; that it exists as a safe and nurturing atmosphere;

that it is frustratingly in the way; that it is a hole into which we will one day disappear – are all driven, ultimately, by our fear and denial of this fundamental, sacred relationship to space.

It should not be surprising, then, that it is largely fear and denial of space that we communicate to our children.

2

ABOVE AND BELOW

| 1 |

I was recently fortunate enough to take a two-day class with Philippe Petit, the virtuoso wirewalker who, on the morning of August 7, 1974, when he was merely twenty-four years old, famously and illegally rigged a wire between the roofs of the World Trade Center towers and then walked back and forth across it eight times.

I was not at the class to learn about wirewalking, although that was what the class was about. I was there to learn about space from someone who clearly has a genius's understanding of it.

I did not learn exactly what I came for. I learned that wirewalking is difficult.

I stumbled through class as best I could, trying to be game, as PP, as I called him in my head, imparted to us various details of the wirewalker's art and asked us to trek several times across the elevated wire – thankfully, only seven feet up – in the dance studio in Brooklyn where the class was taking place.

We did one exercise, however, that made my ears perk up.

In it, PP asked each of us to take a prop – if we were, say, jugglers, this would be a ball or club – and formulate a move that would serve as a way of greeting it, of grounding oneself with it, and of waking it up.

As a writer, I suppose that my true prop would have been my computer, but I did not have the balls to try to work my computer into class, or to mention my art at all in proximity to such a master; I chose one of the white juggling balls he offered without comment.

As we stood there with our props, he reminded us that these greetings we were creating could be very simple.

As I was figuring out how to say hello to my ball in a meaningful way, I was smiling, and I thought: *This does not seem stupid to me. Why?*

I thought of my Italian design heroes, in particular the men and women who have designed for Alessi, and how they understand that objects have spirits and that it is worth the time and energy to create, for instance, a sugar pourer that is shaped like a standing, smiling, neon-colored human breast.

These designers understand the significance of greeting the object. More important, they realize that most of us fail to do this – not out of laziness but out of a lack of consciousness – and they work to change this situation by creating objects that overtly and unmistakably greet us. This, to my mind, is not frivolous; all the friendly, huggable saltshakers and paper-towel holders in the Italian kitchen store are nothing less than heroic attempts to change human perspective. This is art in the same league as painting and poetry.

Every time you hold the sugar pourer over the hot coffee and calibrate the amount of sugar you want in the cup, you and the sugar pourer are one. This is part of what PP knew and demonstrated when he stepped onto the wire with his life attached to a balancing pole – a stick – a quarter of a mile above downtown Manhattan one summer morning in the 1970s.

Fiddling with my ball, trying to solve the problem of the exercise, I thought of my daughter, who was almost two at that point and who said hello – a squealing, delighted "Hi!" – to all things animate and inanimate; who greeted with equal and unmitigated pleasure live puppies, stuffed puppies, and dog poop on the sidewalk.

Why do we ever stop saying "Hi!" to everything? How is the understanding that the entire world is worthy of conscious consideration ever lost?

In class, we took turns demonstrating our moves.

I nervously popped my ball lightly from one hand to the other, an almost nothing gesture.

PP nodded approvingly.

| 2 |

Several months ago, I was looking online for a bathtub ring to put my baby daughter in. I had given away our old one. The ring is a pretty standard baby object, I thought, with a simple design. The baby sits on a plastic disk, which adheres to the floor of the bathtub with suction cups. Three columns, one in between the baby's legs, arise from the disk and support a doughnut-shaped piece of plastic that encircles the baby's torso under her armpits. The apparatus basically operates like scaffolding to help wobbly infants sit upright while they are bathed in the tub.

I could not find this product for sale; instead, I found a new version of it. It was the same bath ring by the same maker, only it had been "improved" with a huge appendage: a long, thick plastic arm that affixed the doughnut top of the bath ring to the lip of the bathtub. The arm was strangely anthropomorphic. Why did the manufacturers put this giant prosthetic arm on my bath ring? I wondered.

In my Google search for *baby bath ring,* I found a document that explained it. It was entitled "Consumers Union Comments to Consumer Product Safety Commission on Staff Briefing Package Recommendations on Baby Bath Seats." The Consumers Union (CU), the nonprofit publisher of *Consumer Reports* magazine, issued the comments "in response to the Consumer Federation of America's July 2000 petition to ban baby bath seats, a petition that argued that they pose an unreasonable risk of death and injury to children." Curious about this risk, I read the paper, which included their baby-product guide's warning to parents not to buy the very bathtub seat I was searching for.

> A typical scenario: A baby is left playing in the seat when someone comes to the front door or the telephone rings. The mother believes the seat will protect her baby. She walks away and is gone briefly. The baby

reaches over to retrieve a toy or tries to stand up. The suction on the bottom pops loose. The baby falls forward or slips. In a few minutes, the mother returns to find her baby face-down in the tub. But by then, it's too late.

I was surprised. The problem with the above scenario, to my mind, was not the bath seat. It was the mother's belief that the seat would "protect her baby" while she was gone. I kept reading, looking for whatever else might be wrong with the seat. Finally, I was stopped short by the following concluding sentence:

"While this CU Guide warns parents never to leave a child alone, it also acknowledges reality: a parent can become distracted, and a child should not have to pay with her or his life as a result."

This sentence gave me pause. If parents are distracted while bathing infants in the bathtub, it is because they do not understand the risk of putting a tiny child who can't yet sit up in water. A mature and respectful relationship with water – let alone with baby – includes this understanding.

What kind of reality is this, where a parent should be protected from having to face the fact that water is precious and perilous, where she should be encouraged to entrust her baby's life – this would be funny if it weren't so sad – to a bath seat? Who is the child here? And what is being protected? It is not, ultimately, the baby. It is the parent's "right" to become distracted.

It is indeed work to give a tiny baby a bath, to be present with her in the phase when she can't sit up, when the soap is slippery, when the water can easily scald her. It is work that requires attention, that requires Be Here Now–ness because of that pesky death problem again.

Be Here Now was a mantra of the 1960s; these days, I think we might, realistically, need to simplify the goal a bit: Be Here. And with that goal, we may finally begin to ask ourselves the question: Where are we?

| 3 |

Daily, inevitably, we submitted to Yelena's increasingly ambitious itinerary for us. She waited about a week – Mick and I were not getting up at three in the morning anymore; we were sleeping until maybe five – before she took us to the place that I believe had been her goal from the beginning. She wouldn't tell us anything about it except that it was a playground; she hoped we liked it; not many foreigners knew about it; and she and Chuck had a nickname for it: Savage Park.

Carrying our snacks, water bottles, wipes, money, cameras, phones, clothes, comic books, and toys, Frank and I and the boys dutifully waddled behind her to the train.

Just as the Diana Ross Playground is located in the larger Central Park, Savage Park, aka Hanegi Playpark, is located in a larger park called Hanegi Koen. It took us a while to get to Savage Park because we had to walk past several other playgrounds within Hanegi Koen, and given that half our ranks were age five or less, we could not easily walk past a playground.

The first playground we stopped at was a fairly traditional

one, with the safety surfacing and the brightly colored immo-
bile play equipment that we were familiar with. The second
playground, located closer to the center of the park, was less
modern but more compelling to the boys. It was essentially
an S-shaped, four-foot-deep concrete canal spanned by a series of arching, metal monkey-bar bridges.

We four adults — Yelena's husband, R, was off from work
that day and joined us — sat and watched as the boys climbed
in, around, and above the canal.

After an hour, we lured the children out of the playground
with gummy candy. The eight of us continued walking, first
up a slight dirt hill, then past a gaggle of unlocked bicycles.

As we walked, we smelled it: smoke.

The smell became stronger as we went ahead. We followed
it until at last we were all standing beside a traditional Japanese hut that was perched atop a downward-sloping one-acre
patch of dirt and trees.

KOJI TAKIGUCHI

Hanegi Playpark

The hut's front porch was completely overflowing with crap, including a pink-painted piano at which a girl, five, was sitting and playing a John Cage–ian ditty. It was a strangely radiant sound to be hearing as we stood there looking down through the smoke – we could see it as well as smell it now – to the smoke's source: open fires.

There were three of them. At one, a boy about eight years old was kneeling, poking at the flames with paper fans; at another, a father was sitting and roasting marshmallows with his toddler son. A third fire seemed to be unattended.

Frank and I turned to look at Yelena, who had stepped to one side and was smiling twinklingly at us.

We turned back and stood there, dumbfounded, staring at the dirt and trees and the structures that were woven around and between them, structures that were clearly not made in any place where safety surfacing had ever been a subject of serious discussion. These were structures that looked like what remained when my sons decided to build an airport out of Legos and then abandoned the project halfway through, only these half-made baggage carts and control towers were much larger and crafted not from nicely interlocking plastic rectangles but from scraps of wood and nails.

This was possible because (as our boys would soon discover), the materials to make the structures – hammers, wood, saws, hole punchers, screwdrivers, nails, paint, brushes, and donated scraps of all kinds – were available at the playpark for everyone to use.

The boys took off running.

Frank and I stumbled after our children. The ground was uneven; the park did not seem to be landscaped in any recog-

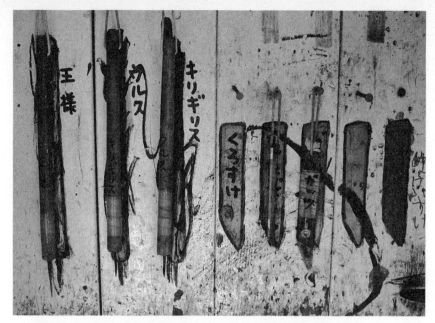

Hole punches and box cutters hanging in the playpark toolshed. I found out later that the writing on the wall is each tool's name and that the tools are named in part to endear them to the children, so instead of "Go find your tools and return them to the shed," the children hear, "Go find Blackie! Blackie needs to come home!"

nizable way. There was dirt underfoot, one presumed, because grass could not possibly survive the trampling; likewise, there were trees around the area because that's where they grew.

Frank had followed Mick. I caught up to King. The man who had been roasting marshmallows over the fire with his son walked toward us, smiling, and extended two freshly marshmallowed sticks.

King and I bowed and smiled and sat down with him and his boy and began the type of conversation we were getting rather good at, where a feeling of camaraderie was engendered by an exchange of only three words: *New, York,* and *Yankees.*

Mick and Chuck wielding hammers on a platform, Hanegi Playpark

King and Chuck on the platform, Mick underneath, Hanegi Playpark

KOJI TAKIGUCHI

A place to sit and rest, Hanegi Playpark

We were sitting on a log about halfway down the slope, facing the way we had come. It was then that I realized that at the top of the slope, I had been so busy looking down – at the fires, the smoke, the tricky ground, and where I was stepping – that I hadn't looked anywhere else. It was only now, when we were sitting, nodding, saying our words, and eating marshmallows, that I thought to look up and around.

Hanegi Playpark

I looked up at the trees. I was astonished to see that there were children in them.

The more I looked, the more children I saw. There were children fifteen feet high in the air. There were children perched on tiny homemade wooden platforms, like circus ladies dressed in glittery clothes about to swan-dive into little buckets. There were children sitting up there, relaxed, in their navy blue sailor-type school uniforms, chatting and eating candy on bitty rectangles of rickety wood as if they were lounging on the Lido deck of the *Love Boat*.

There were children in creaky homemade structures like this in the trees all over the park. There were children, preteens, crouching fifteen feet up on the roof of the playpark hut and then – I gasped to see this – leaping off it onto a pile of ancient mattresses.

King and I sat there on the log, eating warm, white goo.

We were in the park. The park was around us, and the people were around us, and the trees were around us, and the dirt was around us, and the smoke, and the music, and the crisp fall air was around us. The children were around us. The children were in the trees, in the smoke, in the air around us. The children were hanging out; the children were flying in the air around us.

We stayed there as long as we could.

| 4 |

Of all the bumbling and somewhat humiliating experiences I had as a writer-interloper in a wirewalking class with a genius, there was one moment that stands out as neither bumbling nor humiliating, but sublime.

It happened at the end of the first day of class. PP pointed to the wire that was carefully suspended overhead and said that, as the last activity of the day, we would have our "baptismal walk."

I was about to have a heart attack – I had realized rather quickly that, although I would not call myself uncoordinated, I do not have anything near the physical capabilities required to be a wirewalker of even the lowest sort – until PP explained what this meant: he would walk across the wire with his balancing pole, and each of us would walk behind him, one at a time, with our hands on his shoulders and a safety harness on.

I exhaled. *Okay,* I thought. *I can handle that.*

I did not think it was going to be a big deal, walking behind PP, world-famous, never-falling wirewalker, with a safety harness on, a harness secured by PP's gentle giant of an assistant, Zaire.

After deciding that it was highly unlikely that I would die, I basically reverted to autopilot, and I wound up pulling a maneuver not unlike that of the distracted owner of the aforementioned baby bath seat. Death will not get me here, in this particular place, I'd thought. There, I'm done. I'm done thinking about or even paying attention to whatever else it is that will happen.

If you had asked me: What do you think it will be like, walking across a tightrope, seven feet up, behind master wirewalker Philippe Petit?, I probably would have told you, unmoved: It will be like walking.

This would be a nervous, distracted, afraid-to-die person's way of talking.

What is walking, anyway? I see a bag of potato chips on the table. I am a head, disembodied, floating toward a crinkly bag of salty, fatty goodness.

Must.

Get.

Chips.

This is what walking is like, sometimes.

I was standing on the small wooden platform behind PP, who was also standing, only with one foot on the platform and one foot on the wire. I had my hands on PP's shoulders. He did not have his hands on me. He was holding his twenty-foot balancing pole against his waist.

He was wearing his class uniform: a black sleeveless shirt and black pants. I was wearing sweatpants and a T-shirt. It was a hot day, even for August in the city. The dance studio had no AC. We were sweating. I could smell him, human-flowery.

I shifted my weight on my feet a bit up there, trying to find something.

There was no finding anything.

I stood still.

PP seemed to have been waiting for this settling. With his back to me, in his French accent, he asked me, gently: "Shall we go?"

He had already told us that he reserved the right not to take someone on the wire for a baptismal walk for any one of a variety of reasons: if the person was obese, or drunk, or not in the right frame of mind. What the right frame of mind was, he did not explain, but I think it is safe to say we assumed – there were four students in class besides me – that we all had it.

He noted, however, that this same privilege was also ours: we could refuse the baptismal walk if we wanted. And that's why, after all the preparation was done, after we had observed how the cable, which had been fashioned specifically to PP's specifications for this class, was rigged securely and under appropriate tension; after each of us had clambered more or less awkwardly up the ladder to the wooden platform, put the safety harness on, checked that the harness was completely buckled, tested the harness, and seen that Zaire held it firmly; after all of that, in the final moment, PP asked each student this question: "Shall we go?"

And in this asking, he reminded us that after all he had done to make this walk possible (which was to say, pretty much everything) we still held tremendous power in it, because, despite the magnitude of his efforts in relation to our own, it was possible for the two of us to do this action together only if each one of us, individually, first did something alone that was internal, and invisible, and this was agree to fly with him with the understanding that we could do this – the impossible – only because we had surrendered to him in a way that was not meek and resentful but assertive and glad.

"Yes," I said.

The walk was, in this way, very intimate, although there was very little physical contact between us.

And when it was over, it struck me that this question – Shall we go? – and the very particularly pitched assent would be an excellent text for a wedding ceremony. It was so much better than, for instance, the trembly *I will*s Frank and I had said, and not even to each other but to a guy, as nice as he was, whom we never saw again.

Frank and I saying "Shall we go?" to each other and then starting to walk would have been so much more powerful, in some ways, than my asking no questions at all and just saying "Yes" to someone who was not even Frank, a guy asking a question with big words in it, words like *love* and *honor,* words whose meanings we will be discovering all our lives, and then, after having said yes to these giant words, both of us standing there, waiting for the never-to-be-seen-again guy to say, It's okay to kiss, as if kissing in front of friends because a stranger told us to was an appropriate coda to having made the most gigantic vow we would probably ever make.

I suppose this is really just a fuss about language, however, and of course marriage ceremonies as we have created them are mostly about language. What if marriages were not about language but about action? What if dancing, for instance, were not merely the way to celebrate the wedding but the wedding itself? Or what if the wedding action was not dancing, but an everyday action? What if a marriage, which is about beginning an epic lifelong being-together, began by two people being together, not in any way that is supposed to evoke the concept of epic-ness, but just by being together in exactly the kind of regular, everyday way they might be together for thousands and thousands of days? What if couples began their epic being-together by walking around? By sitting down? By stopping for a lemonade?

It's funny that now, writing this, I realize that I know someone whose wedding was exactly like that: Yelena's.

She had a summer wedding ceremony with R that I dismissed at the time as being kind of nuts. In it, she and R asked their guests to meet them on the sidewalk in front of their apartment, which was at Amsterdam and Ninety-Fifth, above the illustrious New York City baby-supply store Albee Baby, and from there, they would all make their way — not necessarily as a mob but as a group that ebbed and flowed, with stops for beer or snacks or a rest or shopping or whatever — to a triangle in Tribeca, where the marriage vows were to be said four or five hours later.

After that, everyone was invited to get on a yellow school bus Yelena and R had rented that would take everyone to Yelena's parents' house in Long Island, where there would be feasting, drinking, and dancing until the wee hours.

I thought that this was crazy. People who are getting married should think about their guests, I fumed. A wedding should be in a sheltered, comfortable place with a heating/cooling system, abundant snacks, and sufficient bathrooms.

Frank and I skipped the walk. Late in the afternoon, we got into a cab with King, who was a toddler at the time, and met the wedding party at the triangle where the ceremony was taking place.

I could not hear the vows; I was chasing King around the traffic island and keeping him from darting in front of cars. Then Frank chased him while I waited in line to greet the bride and groom.

As I hugged Yelena, she whispered in my ear that she was pregnant. She was very early on, with Chuck. The shock of her news pushed me out of myself and caused me to see my-self, hugging her, from the outside. I saw us as if I were look-ing down from a tree branch overhead, where I had noticed a sparrow. I watched from up there, my head cocked to one side, as she transformed herself in my tentative embrace into two people.

In class, I walked across the wire with my hands resting lightly on PP's shoulders.

We took our time. It was easy; we glided. It was like riding on the shoulders of a giant crow.

I left class quickly, alone, and ran down to the subway, where I sat on the gray plastic seat like a giant devotional candle, with the rope of the wick hanging down my back and the flame dancing on top of my head.

3

WHAT THERE IS TO SEE

| 1 |

I was wandering around the kids' section of Muji, the giant Japanese clothing/home/design store, where Frank and the boys and I had followed Yelena one morning.

I was looking at toys. In particular, I was agonizing over whether to buy one of several unusual sets of blocks. Each set had the shapes needed to construct a specific world-famous landmark, and I was leaning, like the Tower of Pisa (which was, sadly, not represented), toward the Taj Mahal.

I was pushing Mick, who was asleep in the stroller. Frank was wandering around somewhere with King. I was relatively free.

I had been browsing around for a while when I realized

that I had lost track of Yelena. We had entered the kids' section together; where had she gone? I circled around the entire section again and found her, sitting on the floor, her legs in a wide V, next to a display of toddler clothing. She was surrounded by art materials she had just bought: a beautiful colored-pencil set and several blank sketchpads. She was cutting some paper out of one of the books with brand-new red scissors.

Chuck was exploring some toys nearby. Gen, Yelena and R's one-year-old, was out with his babysitter.

R was not around. He was having a medical procedure done that day.

Yelena was sitting on the floor of the Muji store making an illustrated book for R.

She spent at least forty-five minutes sitting there. I even left Mick sleeping in the stroller next to her for a few minutes and went to get a café au lait in the Muji-aurant.

At the time, I did not think much about what she was doing, beyond that it was a little odd that she was sitting in the middle of the store and that it was nice that she was making something for R.

But making something wasn't all she was doing. She was also taking something. She walked into a giant, anonymous department store and turned it into her very own personal daycare center/art studio. She left that capitalist mecca with something she took the time – the space! – to sit down and make, using the store's art supplies (which she paid for) and using the store's shiny display objects (which she did not) as distractions to keep her four-year-old (to say nothing of her four tiresome guests) occupied.

She went into a humongous store, paid for a small number of art supplies, and stole time and space.

It was action as architecture: a fantastic, creative, political act.

I didn't see it then.

| 2 |

We did not, in fact, return to Savage Park on that trip. There were too many other things to do, places to go. But the rest of the trip was, in a sense, a denouement. I spent the remainder of our time in Japan, and, really, months after that, waiting to go back to Savage Park alone.

How and when I could do that, I didn't know, but it was there, an inkling: everywhere else I went in Japan, I believed, somehow, in the face of all good sense and the reality of my family life, that time and space, alone and apart, in Savage Park was a possibility that was waiting for me.

| 3 |

On our second and final day of class, right before our last trek across the wire, Philippe Petit gave us a wirewalking demonstration.

It was a relief to sit and watch him and not have to do anything scary and physical. We arranged ourselves in a line on the floor, parallel to the wire, and looked up at him.

PP stood on the platform, holding his balancing pole.

He stepped on the wire. I watched his body change with that step. His back suddenly had a different quality to it, as if

Frank and Mick, Hanegi Playpark

someone had plugged his spine into an unseen power source, and it was now glowing, neon orange.

He bounced up and down on the wire, gracefully and lightly, like a ballerina performing entrechats.

You must remember that this was a miracle: He was not a dancer *en pointe*. He was a solid, middle-aged man standing on a seven-eighths-of-an-inch-wide cable seven feet in the air holding a twenty-foot-long pole. Yet he did this Tinker Bell spring not once, not twice, but several times before proceeding forward.

He had told us he was going to show us a procession of his signature movements; his vocabulary of the wire, so to speak.

When I see an artist on a high wire, I imagine his idea is to emphasize his lightness; to twirl, for example, a little paper parasol above his head. PP says bah to that. The images he has created for the wire are remarkably grounded: a field laborer walking home after a day's work; lying down and taking a rest, practically a nap, on the wire; kneeling; and saluting the sky.

This last one in particular seemed to me a hallmark of his mastery. He understands that, even wildly, spectacularly alone, soaring beyond where any reasonable man would ever go, he is not, as the kids say, all that; he is no Icarus. There is always the awareness in his work that there is more. As singular and solitary as his art is, his entire body of work gestures toward something greater. The fact that he is artist-in-residence at the Cathedral Church of St. John the Divine makes perfect sense, although his work is not explicitly religious in any way.

When class was over, I ventured to ask him about that little bounce I had seen him do when he first stepped on the wire: What was that?

He was busily clearing his notes from the table, where he had set them for the day. He did not look at me as he explained that it was his way of saying hello to the wire, his wanting to feel it, and it was also, he said, making eye contact with me for just a second: joy.

After all his years of practice, three hours a day, every day, after all that self-discipline, that insane amount of rigor and tenacity. I thought: *Amazing. The man still plays.*

| 4 |

On the day before we left, Yelena gave us a gift. Frank and I had just gotten up and were sitting around on the still-reclining red-and-yellow couches with our coffees in hand when she announced that she was planning to take all four boys back to the Junk Playground for the day so that Frank and I could go to a love hotel.

We looked at her.

Yes, yes, she told us – love hotels are perfectly clean, they're respectable, you will have fun, you will have a great time. Some have microphones!

We looked at each other.

You know, for karaoke!

We all laughed.

Yelena gave us directions to a street where there were a bunch of them.

Go ahead, she said.

We went.

| 5 |

A very good resource for someone who is interested in going to a playpark and picking up a hammer and nails and pounding away at scraps of crap to make something is the work of the nineteenth-century British writer John Ruskin.

I tripped over the following line in Ruskin's *On Art and Life,* a contemporary repackaging of two of his essays, "The Nature of Gothic" and "The Work of Iron, in Nature, Art, and Policy."

In this passage, he offers a moving plea for allowing men – in particular, the men who built the Gothic cathedrals of the age – to be, as he says, "fully men" and not mere tools of the architect; to be allowed to use their imaginations in their work, to be allowed to make mistakes.

He wrote:

> Let him but begin to imagine, to think, to try and do anything worth doing; and the engine-turned precision is lost at once. Out come all his roughness, all his dulness, all his incapability; shame upon shame, failure upon failure, pause after pause: but out comes the whole majesty of him also; and we know the height of it only when we see the clouds settling upon him. And whether the clouds be bright or dark, there will be transfiguration behind and within them.

In this, written more than a hundred and fifty years ago, he articulated why my modern-day love of Savage Park was so immediate. It wasn't just that the children were flying in the air there, it wasn't just that they were making insanely great structures, it wasn't just that the playpark hut was a junk lover's dream. It was because the place existed at all for just this reason: this full and complete allowance of a self, including all the ineptness, failure, and possibility of death, because it is understood that only with this allowance do we have the capacity to be great.

When I went back a year later, I stood in Savage Park alone and considered it: the four-year-old boys swinging hammers into tree stumps, bending nails sideways into wood scraps, for no reason, necessarily; or for fun; or for the purpose of making something interesting; or for the sheer delight of feeling the force.

A place to sit and rest, Hanegi Playpark

I didn't know it then, as I stood there surrounded by foreign people and foreign language, that this was not a new
and exotic topography or that Ruskin, an Englishman, had, in
his way, mapped this landscape more than a century earlier
when he listed the six characteristics of Gothic architecture,
and the first, above all others, above changefulness, natural-
ism, grotesqueness, rigidity, and redundancy, was savageness.

| 6 |

Frank and I walked holding hands, like buddied-up children
on a field trip, into the practically funereal black-marble entrance of the love hotel, where we, somehow, with gestures
and pointing and displays of money, negotiated with the fishy
lady behind the Plexiglas window for a stay of three hours.

We knew we had done this when she pushed a key through
the slot.

Frank held the key as we went up the elevator and down
the hall to the room with a number on the door that matched
the number on the key.

Frank put the key in the lock and opened the door.

We walked into the room, where there was, of course, a
bed, made up nicely with bright, white linens, and a bath-
room with an exceptionally – even for Japan – outfitted toilet,
a toilet that, like the finest toddler-princess toilets available
here, played tinkly music when you put your bare bottom on
its pink seat and peed.

And there was also a box near the headboard of the bed
that functioned as a shelf. At a fine American hotel, you might
expect to see in it a shiny magazine – the *World of Interiors,*

say – rolled up carefully so that it might be unrolled and gazed at. But here, instead of a rolled-up magazine to contemplate, there were two sparkly silver microphones to hold, two microphones resting in two matte silver cylinders that were built into the box, two microphones sitting like beer cans in their cozies, and there were cords from the mikes that disappeared into the box so that a human voice that had, perhaps tentatively, made the leap between human lips and microphone head could, from there, be snaked farther through the microphone cord, to the place behind the box and below the bed, and from there even farther, to the giant TV hanging on the wall across from the bed, so that the human voice that went into the microphone quietly and alone could come out of the sound system loud and layered on top of and around and under another human voice, a voice that was singing a song that was recorded elsewhere, long ago, a song that, through the miracle of global sound distribution, was now so well known that people all over the world, even the ones who don't speak the language, know this song, know Michael Jackson's "Don't Stop 'Til You Get Enough," and everyone could sing this song with Michael Jackson here, in this time- and space-bending capsule of a room, even though Michael Jackson was not technically here in this room, or even in a body on earth anymore.

Frank and I and no one else were on the white plain of the bed together.

When we consider space and our human place in it, we use the wrong sense. We use our eyes. We look at things. This is ridiculous.

Space belongs to the ears, to hearing, to the ebb and flow

of invisible waves, to music, to speech, to yelling, to singing, to gasping, to silence.

Space is born in the ears and detected in the ears and entered and exited through the moist, circular portal of the ears. Most of us come into space hearing; in the womb, our eyes closed, we are hearing. Many of us die hearing; some say it is the last sense to go.

When I am in a love hotel, not fully understanding where I am, with my husband doing this old activity that continues to mystify and amaze me, I am not seeing. I am not even sure I am touching, smelling, or tasting. I am being touched. I am listening. I am listening to something beyond the sounds of myself, my husband, and the room.

I am listening so that it becomes a way of exploring. I am listening my way into an invisible palace, where each room is more wondrous than the last, and in each room I am coming closer to the one room, which is secret, where there is majesty, where entering and leaving space is fully possible.

Frank and I lay together on the bed, the microphones lying silently in their silver cozies overhead like mummies in their tombs.

We got up and got dressed.

Eventually Frank said, "Ready?" By which he meant, "Shall we go?"

| 7 |

I came back from our trip to Japan and began reading about play; I was trying to make sense of Hanegi Playpark. I was

Girls playing, Hanegi Playpark

thinking that if I understood how the word *play* is defined in the United States, I would understand why we make playgrounds here that look the way they do.

I read for a while. What I found in reading is that play has been viewed primarily as an activity and that one of the primary goals in writing about this activity has been to explain its function.

My favorite writer on the topic was probably Roger Caillois, whose seminal book on play, *Man, Play, and Games* (1961), does not attempt to define the reason behind play so much as trace its slippery territory.

Play is free, separate, uncertain, unproductive, governed by rules, and make-believe, he wrote. Yet he also added, brilliantly, "The structures of play and reality are often identical, but the respective activities that they subsume are not reducible to each other in time or place. They always take place in domains that are incompatible."

Play, as Caillois saw it, might completely mimic reality, but it was not reality. It was a reality twin.

| 8 |

I remember being with Yelena and her boys at another aquarium she took us to, Tokyo Sea Life Park. This was near the end of the trip, but my jet lag was still intense.

We were sitting in a small amphitheater in the lowest level of the aquarium, looking at the shark tank. There was a lounge area there with vending machines so that one could sit comfortably and watch the sharks' spectacular zooms while lazily drinking bottled water and chomping dried fish crackers.

I sat there with Mick, who had his head in my lap and who was also beginning to fade.

I wanted, more than anything, to sleep, and I was acutely aware of the fact that I could not, and I also could not, I felt, just say this, because I was a guest. (I would realize on my second trip to Japan how very Japanese this thinking was when I went to a dinner with a dozen new Japanese friends and watched two twentysomething guests who had been out all night partying the night before sit at the table with their bobbing heads propped up in their hands as they dozed, preferring to do that rather than go home, and everyone else at the table understanding this, that being present but asleep was preferable to admitting exhaustion and being absent, and so ignored their sleeping and did not comment as their heads lolled precariously over their paper-umbrella'd drinks.)

Sitting upright there with Mick, dying to collapse, I was chafing at the perceived constraints of my guest status when Yelena, a playmaker who knows a thing or two about theater and what is possible there, walked over and sat down beside us in the amphitheater stands.

She looked around genially and said, "Wouldn't this be a nice place to take a nap?" And then she lay down and closed her eyes, as if this were something we could actually do.

I was galled by this. What was her understanding of her place in the world, I harrumphed, that she thought that what amounted to a public park bench, this one with passersby showing their terrifying teeth, was a safe place to enter the murky, vulnerable state of sleep?

But as soon as I asked the question, I knew: she thought the street was an appropriate place to get married; she thought a department store was an appropriate place to make art; she conducted herself, in some respects, like a homeless person, not because she was homeless but because she was always at home, and this was a quality I admired her for immensely.

| 9 |

Play is not something that we do; it is something that we are. It is the state of consciousness that we are born with, and it gradually diminishes in power as we age, until, as adults, we generally find that we are able to enter and exit this state with ease only if we have practiced.

Slide, Hanegi Playpark

Our adult relationship to play may vary widely. We may choose never to play; we may never realize that the option to play is open to us; we may take shortcuts in the form of drugs or alcohol to enter a simulacrum of the play state; or we may discover that we want to, and can, play all the time, even when we are supposedly working.

Play is ultimately less of a what and more of a how. Yet we do not generally think of play like this; we think of play as being a stereotypically playful-looking action performed primarily by children, and we put this play action in context by defining it as not-work. So we don't so much define *play* itself; we define *play* by emphasizing the importance of work in relation to it. For example, we tell children that they must stop playing and do homework, and then, eventually, like Mom and Dad, get work (a job).

And yet: We are here for only a short time; we are going to die. How will you live your life? is really the only important question there is, and *playfully* is one of the most courageous, most generous, and most fully human ways to answer this question.

| **10** |

In "The Nature of Gothic," Ruskin wrote:

> And therefore, while in all things that we see or do, we are to desire perfection, and strive for it, we are nevertheless not to set the meaner thing, in its narrow accomplishment, above the nobler thing, in its mighty progress; not to esteem smooth minuteness above shattered majesty; not to prefer mean victory to honourable defeat; not to lower the level of our aim, that we may more surely enjoy the complacency of success. But, above all, in our dealings with the souls of other men, we are to take care how we check, by severe requirement or narrow caution, efforts which might otherwise lead to a noble issue; and still more, how we withhold our admiration from great excellencies, because they are mingled with rough faults.

Given all the things I saw in Hanegi Playpark, all the astonishing gewgaws the children made, I do not know that I could choose a favorite if I were ever able to curate my own exhibit with all those wonders.

But there was one that I loved dearly. It was set at the northwest corner of the park, at the bottom of the slope. From the outside it looked a bit like the piles of cardboard boxes stacked up for recycling in front of my apartment building in New York.

Noriko, the head play worker at the park who was my hostess, roommate, employer, babysitter, protector, and tormentor during the miraculous week when I returned to Tokyo alone a year after our visit with Yelena, revealed the thing to me as we were picking up upturned nails and other hazardous bits along the park's north end.

She gestured toward what was actually a clubhouse, saying that even in this playpark – this somewhat secret, wild place – the children still had a need to create a place that was even more secret, even more wild.

I admired the clubhouse. Assembled from wood scraps, boxes, and crap, it was essentially a miniature of Savage Park itself.

Finally Noriko pointed out a feature of the clubhouse I hadn't recognized.

"Toyet," she said, chuckling.

It took me a few seconds to understand.

It was a twelve-foot piece of bamboo that had been sliced in half and turned cup-upward, and it was supported on one end with a network of sticks and branches so that if you were seven years old and standing in front of it, it would be just under waist-high. This conglomeration of sticks and branches served as rigging, supporting the bamboo trough so that it

Exterior of clubhouse, Hanegi Playpark

sloped down gently, eventually touching ground just beyond where the plywood walls of the clubhouse ended.

It was a toilet: a graceful piece of engineering. And the added beauty of it was that the spot where you (if you were a seven-year-old boy) were meant to stand with your penis out and begin the peeing process was right under the lookout window, which had been cut out of the cardboard wall. One could stand there peeing and simultaneously enjoying a broad and yet concealed view of the playpark's north end.

I tried to imagine it: a seven-year-old boy standing at the window of his secret clubhouse looking out at his domain while peeing in a toilet of his own making, recognizing the greatness of his place within a place that is still greater.

That Hanegi Koen has very clean bathrooms – luxurious ones, compared to the public bathrooms in New York City – a ninety-second walk from this clubhouse is unimportant.

4

SAVAGE PARK

| 1 |

The vast majority of American playgrounds cannot look anything like Hanegi Playpark, not because we don't love play in America or because we don't have good intentions for our children or because we don't love building with tools, or because we don't love trees, fires, and pianos.

American playgrounds can't look like Hanegi Playpark because Americans refuse to make peace with their own death and dying. This approach is built into the culture at the most profound levels, and the mostly unconscious indoctrination into this perspective begins very young.

Mick playing, Hanegi Playpark

| 2 |

I came home from that first visit to Tokyo with my family and began, like a girl with a lingering crush, to do Internet searches on Hanegi Playpark regularly, just to see what would come up. For months, it was nothing.

And then one day, there was a website, and then another day, the website had been expanded, with a page that had a form you could fill out and then send.

I had no idea what the form was for, or where, exactly, I was sending it to – the site was written entirely in Japanese – but I typed into the form that I was a writer from New York City working on a book about Hanegi Playpark, and were there any employees there who spoke English who could write me back?

In a few days, I heard from Noriko. In her not perfect but still comprehensible English, she wrote that she was the head play worker in the park, and, indeed, in some of the pictures I took of the boys on that first day we went to the playpark, I can now pick her out in the background.

In the back-and-forth after that initial e-mail, I eventually told her that I wanted to come to Tokyo to shadow her at work for a week. Her unabashed and open yes – followed by a fortuitous meeting between her and Yelena at the playpark

Noriko leading her bike up the steps of Hanegi Koen on her way to Hanegi Playpark

(*She's really cool, Fuss,* Yelena e-mailed me) – emboldened me to ask if I could also stay with her.

That she said yes to my staying in her home for a week, never having met me, was wildly generous, especially when I realized, once she met me at the subway station after my long flight (straight from NYC this time, no layover) and took me to her place, that her entire apartment was about the size of Mick and King's train table. We slept there, side by side, on the floor, in a way I haven't done since the days of my very first sleepovers, at nine years old, in my sleeping bag, which

Frank and King, moments after arriving in Hanegi Playpark.
Noriko is in the triangle slightly to the left and over King's head.

was orange and printed with a picture of Snoopy asleep on top of his doghouse and Woodstock standing on his belly, awake, and the text *One of us always stays awake in case of vampires.*

I was the Woodstock on that trip. Noriko and I spent twelve-hour days, on average, at the playpark, and I was, there was no doubt about it, working. I was taking notes, talking to people, trying to understand, trying to be understood, trying to be respectful, and trying to play, the last of which I found pretty difficult to do. I was nervous; I was exhausted. I missed my boys. During times when I was supposed to be acting spontaneously, I found my mind blanking.

The perils of my blanking out were brought home to me particularly harshly one night when we were at the playpark quite late, again. The playpark hours were supposed to be 9:00 a.m. to 7:00 p.m., but in reality there were always people hanging out there after-hours – teenagers, predictably – and Noriko, whose job was something along the lines of social worker/handyman/diplomat/nurse/landscaper, routinely did not leave until nine or ten o'clock.

As I wandered around the playpark, I found myself thinking a lot about how to characterize what Noriko did there. She was not a playground worker in any way that I had seen one before.

When I'm at home in New York City, for example, and I see men or women in green-jumpsuit uniforms come to the playground at Forty-Third Street between Eighth and Ninth Avenues, I know what they are there for. They are there to unplug toilets and sweep up gunk, among other manual tasks. And of course they may call the police if something untoward is happening or call 911 if someone is injured, just like any-one else.

But this work is not the same as what Noriko does, which is less of a focus on and fixing of objects (that type of repair can be absurd in a place where all structures are handmade and many are intended to be temporary) than a kind of con-tinual, low-key fussing; not quite like a mother, because a mother wants to keep her children safe and clean; and not quite like a party host, because a host wants to ensure fun; but more like a gardener, because in tending to the health of plants, the gardener tends to the birds, bees, and other ani-mals, as plants, birds, bees, and other animals can't be sep-arated from one another in relation, and ultimately what Noriko does is tend to a space that is acknowledged by every-one to have everything in it.

The playpark has everything in it, including nature in its beauty and treachery; including man-made spaces in their youthful heroism and then inevitable shabby disorder; in-cluding people – old people, adults, teenagers, children, and babies; including fire; including lunch on the fire; and includ-ing the possibility of death. And it takes a particular person to hold all that and to say it is here, and we are here with it, and there is no cleaning it up; there is no point in that. There is only time with it, and what we choose to do in that time, and how we do what we choose to do.

And so, on this particular night, as the sun went down, Noriko told me that we were going to be out extra late, be-cause we were going to play a game in the park called angels and devils. As Noriko explained it, we – *we* meaning Noriko and I and a group of, it appeared to me, about twelve teenage boys – would be using not just the playpark but all of Hanegi Koen, the beautifully landscaped park in which Hanegi Playpark was set, as our field. The whole concept seemed so outlandish that it was hard for me to take in. Surely Noriko will let me be excused from this, I told myself.

But no. There I was, playing game after game of rock, paper, scissors with boy after teenage boy, because it was by playing rock, paper, scissors that we were deciding who was going to be the devil.

And as we transformed our hands, the rules of angels and devils were explained to me, and I was thrown back to a game that I was involved with as a very small child, when I lived in a neighborhood full of kids on a cul-de-sac in a nice town in Connecticut. This game was called war. And although I don't remember anyone getting hurt in this game, which must have been a miracle, I do remember that the entire tone of the street changed when we played it. It was dark, intense, and scary. The stakes were high, and they were real. War involved a lot of secret meetings and yelling insults, which I was a part of, and running around people's houses spying, which I was a part of, and rock-throwing, which I was not a part of. That was handled by the bigger boys. (My Boy Scout–leader father, revealing a Cro-Magnon-esque wisdom I did not fully appreciate until some forty years later, told me when I was a little girl that all I would ever need to know about boys was that they could be divided into two categories: bed-wetters and rock-throwers.) It always took our little community a couple of days to recover after war broke out.

Angels and devils, I feared, was going to be dark like this. The game was essentially a combination of hide-and-seek and tag: one person, the unfortunate loser of the umpteen games of rock, paper, scissors, would be the devil – that is, the seeker. Everyone else was an angel, and angels did not seek, they hid. The angels' goal was to creep back to base – in this case, the playpark hut – without being tagged by the devil or the devil's henchmen, because once you were tagged by the devil, you then had to join him in his search.

I sat there, pumping my fist up and down like an automaton, losing round after round of rock, paper, scissors. I was panicking. I imagined myself as the devil, alone, running around Hanegi Koen in the dark, for hour after interminable hour, trying to tag roving packs of sneaky teenage boys.

And Noriko, finally, seemed to understand the fact that I was not physically or mentally prepared to be the devil, because as my losing streak continued unabated and I entered some zone of doom where I couldn't think properly and could hear a sound in my head like a giant bulldozer backing up, she came over and stood above me, as if pulled by the force of my despair.

I was stuck on one gesture: scissors. I just kept playing scissors. Scissors are sharp, I believe I was thinking. It was as if I had forgotten the logic of the game.

My young opponents, seeing quickly that I was on scissors autopilot, played rock. Time after time I was beaten, and each time, my spiral of panic made yet another terrible curl.

Finally it came down to me and one other boy. He was one of the youngest, probably just ten, and, like me, also panicking. The loser of this game would be the devil.

I heard Noriko bark: "Amy-san, why do you never play paper?"

Paper, I remember thinking in my robot fog. I had forgotten about paper.

I threw a couple of papers in. My young friend, finally, lost.

I walked away from the match with gratitude. Saved.

An hour later, Noriko and I were crouching in some shrubbery along the edge of the park beside a disgruntled-looking stray calico cat. A herd of teenage boys – devils all – came thundering by us. I felt like one of the children hiding from the Nazis in the crypt with Julie Andrews in *The Sound of Music.*

We finally crept back onto the porch of the playpark hut, aka Heaven, where I lay down by the pink piano and thanked God repeatedly.

That was one of the hardest days at any job I ever had.

| 3 |

Some history: According to Hitoshi Shimamura, the International Play Association regional vice president in East Asia, the pilot park that became Hanegi Playpark was founded in 1975. It was modeled on the first adventure playground, which was created by landscape architect Carl Theodor Sørensen and which opened in Emdrup, Copenhagen, in 1943, when that town was under German occupation. According to play researcher Susan Solomon's important book *American Playgrounds: Revitalizing Community Space,* this first-ever adventure playground had, essentially, three components: a vacant lot; donated scraps ("useless fragments of wood, metal, or masonry" and "a few building implements such as hammers, saws, and nails"); and a single adult supervisor, who "was available only for guidance and was key to the success of the playground."

Sørensen's playground, then known as a "junk playground," was the seed for many more. According to adventure-playground advocate Lia Sutton, there are currently about a thousand adventure playgrounds in Europe, largely in Denmark, Switzerland, France, Germany, the Netherlands, and England.

Adventure playgrounds arrived in Britain in the late 1940s and 1950s, where they benefited greatly from a powerfully placed playground advocate, trained horticulturist Lady Allen of Hurtwood. As a result of her zeal, many adventure playgrounds were set up in the British Isles. In the United States, adventure playgrounds simply did not take hold in the same way. Playgrounds themselves began emerging in the United States in the 1880s, when, as noted by Howard Chudacoff in his excellent book *Children at Play: An American History,* the playground movement in the United States began, and "reformers established sand gardens in parks and schoolyards to promote play among very young children." In the early 1900s, the Playground Association of America was founded, and that event marked "the professionalization of playground work." By 1917, the country had 3,940 public and private playgrounds, and it employed 8,768 playground directors.

With the advent of the automobile, the playground served a basic need: it got the children off the streets and out of the way of vehicles. In 1922, automobiles caused the death of an astonishing 477 children in New York City. But during the

Depression, playground funding was cut, and the movement sputtered. The economy improved following World War II, but the public playground's decline continued, because middle-class families provided their children "with their own play accoutrements at home," as Chudacoff noted, and backyard playgrounds competed with public play areas.

In the 1950s, the playground in America began a brief relationship with the art world, because, as Solomon wrote, the connection "between playgrounds and sculpture began to take hold." In 1954, the Museum of Modern Art held a playground-design competition that received significant media attention and heightened the legitimacy of playgrounds in art circles and elsewhere.

The association between playgrounds and art did not last long; safety issues became important, and commercial products filled the playparks. Lady Allen of Hurtwood toured American playgrounds in 1965 and called them "an administrator's heaven and a child's hell."

In the 1970s, with the emergence of an energetic new do-it-yourself movement, homemade play spaces became more compelling. Jeremy Joan Hewes's inspired and inspiring 1975 book *Build Your Own Playground!* focused on the West Coast designs of Jay Beckwith, who incorporated many of the adventure-playground ideas in his instructions for making tunnels and ramps out of rope and discarded materials. It was on the West Coast during that period that one of America's few still-operating, year-round adventure playgrounds was founded: the Berkeley Marina Adventure Playground.

The Berkeley playground opened in 1979, around the same time as Hanegi Playpark, but it is structured somewhat differently than its Japanese counterpart. Whereas Hanegi Playpark is for all ages, Berkeley is meant primarily for children seven and older; younger children are welcome as long as they are kept *"within arm's reach"* of an accompanying adult, administrators state on the playground's website (italics theirs). Also, every child who enters the Berkeley playground must have his parent or guardian sign a waiver releasing the playground from liability for any injuries that might occur there.

The Berkeley playground website tries to prepare parents for the hurdles they will face when they bring their children to the park; its guidelines remind parents to keep their cell phones in their pockets and use good judgment. "If what they are doing is destructive and dangerous," the website advises, "please stop them and cleanup."

In contrast, Hanegi Playpark's advice consists mainly of a sign posted near one playground entrance that reads PLAY FREELY AT YOUR OWN RISK.

It is worth noting that the first line of Solomon's book is "Existing American playgrounds are a disaster." There seem to be indications, however, that play and play spaces are becoming the subject of renewed public interest in the United States. In New York City — where it is against park rules to climb a tree in Central Park — a new type of playground designed by the famed architectural firm Rockwell Associates recently opened near the South Street Seaport. The playground is a hopeful sign: it features loose parts — Rockwell-team-designed foam blocks — as well as sand and water. The playground also employs a play associate who, despite some initial misgivings, has been embraced by the playground's visitors, adult and child alike.

The adventure-playground community is small, and news of this play area, called Imagination Playground, had reached Hanegi Playpark when I was there as Noriko's guest. At one point, the aforementioned Shimamura, who is also a friend of Noriko's, sat beside me and weighed in.

"It seems that Americans have always had problems with risk," he said.

I nodded.

"Even the name of the place . . ." He trailed off, and then, looking at me slyly, pointed to his baseball hat.

"Imagination stays safely in the head," he said.

| 4 |

On my next-to-last night at Hanegi Playpark, Yelena stopped by to visit me. It was such a huge relief to see her: someone from my hood.

Noriko had arranged a sort of party for me in the playpark. She is a musician—she almost always carries a tin whistle in her backpack—and she sings and plays guitar, tin whistle, and accordion with several friends in a band devoted to Irish music called Bailey's Milk.

She gathered the members of Bailey's Milk in the playpark that evening at dusk, and I had the slightly surreal experience of sitting on a log in front of a fire with Yelena as Noriko sang "Down by the Salley Gardens" to us in Japanese-accented English.

It had been a hard workweek for me in the playpark and I was drained by the demands of being a good guest. I sat with Yelena and spoke English and did not pretend to be feeling anything I wasn't as Noriko sang.

Yelena and I did not know it then, but our families were both about to expand: Yelena, who was in the process of divorcing R, would have another baby, a boy she would name Aevi. Frank and I would also have a third baby, a girl we named Katie.

For her part, Noriko, who had just gone through a difficult breakup and was gloomy about her prospects for ever becoming a mother, would marry at six months pregnant in a wildly joyful, crowded ceremony in Hanegi Playpark. She would end up saying her vows with a man named Haruki, a fellow play worker from Nagano, a few feet from where she was at that instant standing and singing her Irish-ish heart out.

Yelena and I did not know any of this. We sat there, in the smoke, and talked to each other out of the sides of our mouths like gangsters.

As we sat there in this landscape we could never have imagined ourselves in, with everything not yet happened to us, I felt some sense of completion. It was like we were finally at the show we had been waiting to see for so long.

| 5 |

Of all the people I met in the playpark, one of my favorites was Ossan. He was in his sixties and had been coming to the park on and off since it opened in the 1970s.

He came twice the week I was there with Noriko. He walked in quietly in the morning, without fanfare, and set up shop for himself at one of the picnic tables. He stood there with a knife, carving *taketumbo* – dragonfly – toys out of soft bamboo.

Taketumbo are essentially little helicopter propellers; you clasp the stem between your palms, then slide one palm against the other quickly and release the stem: the *taketumbo* flies up.

Ossan's being there in the park reminded me in some ways of Yelena on the floor of the Muji store making her book. Ossan just showed up, in his fishing vest and hat, and stood there with his knife, not really talking to anyone but not avoiding anyone either, just working/playing to suit himself.

In this way he made a space for himself in the playpark that was like a space I had seen before in private, in my home, growing up with my dad. My dad had made that masculine, making-things space for himself in a room off the garage. He had it all in there – the tools, the wood, the oils, the gasoline, the light but considered touch – and the objects, new or repaired, emerged miraculously after a long weekend afternoon.

Ossan made what I thought of as a private, male making-things space in a public place. He had his suburban garage in the Tokyo playpark, at the picnic table. One day he was joined by three little girls who were making a potion out of crushed berries.

I smiled every time I looked at Ossan that day he was joined by the girls, thinking how impossible that tableau would be in New York City, imagining how the first-time parents at the Bleecker Street Playground in New York City would respond if a sixty-year-old guy in a fishing vest wandered through the playground gates with a knife and some wood. The parent phones wouldn't be able to dial 911 fast enough.

Ossan gave me two *taketumbo* he made. One is painted brown with orange stripes. The other is plain wood – I watched him make it – and on the propellers is written in ballpoint pen, *Amy / By Ossan*.

They are fragile. I was scared that they would break before I got them home. And though they did survive the journey, which they spent wrapped in my socks, the painted one is cracked from Mick and King playing with it.

I told the boys: These toys are not for playing with anymore. They sit on my bookshelf now and are almost never touched.

| 6 |

When someone is a chef and wields his knife with such sensitivity that the knife is a part of him, we call that mastery. The chef has completely mastered – dominated – the knife; the knife is like an extension of himself. It has become a part of his body.

This has been our understanding of our human relationship with objects for thousands of years. Objects are inanimate until we animate them. We touch them, we hold them in our hands, we use them, we strive for dominance over them. We believe we have achieved this dominance when we have complete control of them, when we can wield the objects with as much sensitivity as if they were a part of us.

This particular idea of dominance, or mastery, over things is interesting because it tends to obscure the fact that the objects we dominate have a corresponding effect on us. When you wield the knife, you become knife-ish: you cut, you slice, you have edges. You yourself are transformed by this relationship with the knife into knife-ishness. The degree to which one is successful in becoming knife-ish stands as a measure of mastery: if one wields a knife with ax-ishness, one has not yet mastered the knife.

We tend to overlook this reciprocal relationship between the object and the self, however. We tend to miss the notion that a master sushi chef who has become thoroughly and sublimely knife-ish may be viewed by the knife as the object that has been dominated.

The reason we don't think of this reciprocal relationship, of course, is that we don't believe that objects have views, per se. We believe that objects are inanimate. They sit there lifeless until we pick them up, and then they are useful or not and we can master them or not according to our desires. All objects are puppets to us in this way.

What a human can do with a puppet is amazing. It was only a mere stick, it bears repeating, that PP held in his hands and used to defy death in his dance a quarter of a mile over Manhattan that August morning. It was a stick that he held to his gut, that he mastered until his sensitivity to it was so great that the stick was a part of him, until his holding the stick to his gut and his becoming the stick were the same, until, in holding the stick to his gut, he became, in fact, very wide in his midsection, with two tiny feet and a tiny head, like a giant bird with his giant wings spread. He became, then, not just stickish but, in an extremely creative use of his stickish-ness, birdish.

This is not to say that every kid playing with a stick will walk between skyscrapers (or even that he or she should want to). But in toying with a stick, a kid is toying with the world in which he and the stick are a part, a world which is itself a combination of forces at play in a way that is so sophisticated that we have barely even begun to explain it.

As game designer Chris Crawford wrote succinctly in his book *The Art of Computer Game Design* way back in 1984:

> The most fascinating thing about reality is how it changes, the intricate webwork of cause and effect by which all things are tied together. The best way to represent this webwork is to allow the audience to explore it fully – to let the audience generate causes and observe effects. [Computer] games provide this interactive experience, and it is a crucial factor of their appeal.

Yet most of us are hardly cognizant of this webwork in real space.

| 7 |

There was no more Irish music in Hanegi Playpark. It was my last day in Tokyo and Noriko was taking me to another park, to a workshop she was running there. She was going to lead a group of volunteers in making a pop-up adventure playground.

I thought it was odd that we weren't taking any tools or other materials with us, but Noriko told me there would be things to work with at the park. She shouldered her cloth backpack and off we went.

The park we arrived at was a somewhat depressing grassy acre in what was essentially a traffic rotary in the shadow of a giant apartment building. On one side, it was bordered by a highway, and on the other side, by a street that served as an artery between the highway and the building.

The only pieces of play equipment there were a metal swing set with one broken swing and a concrete ramp, about six feet high, that seemed meant to be a slide, although I couldn't imagine it being welcoming to anyone's bottom.

In one corner of the park there was a storage shed similar to what one sees in the yards of suburban homes in America. What we were going to use to make the playground was in the storage shed, Noriko told me.

It took a while to figure out how to get in. When Noriko finally located the key and opened the shed, I was surprised: I had expected tools, but there were only a couple of tires, a dolly, some mats, rope, and a few logs that had been sliced in half.

There were about half a dozen volunteers already gathered when we arrived at the park. The number had grown to about a dozen by the time we got the shed open. My understanding was that we had about an hour and a half before crowds of people would begin arriving to play. I did not see how we were going to be able to construct anything meaningful with what we had in ninety minutes. Noriko began by having all of us walk around the park and pick up any sharp or dangerous objects, and while doing so, we were to take note of the landscape, of any interesting features, and of any opportunities for play, given the aforementioned materials we were going to be working with. We did this for about twenty minutes and then regrouped to compare notes.

It was decided pretty quickly that we would build two structures out of rope: a swing, which would be suspended between two trees, and a monkey bridge, or climbing structure, made of two parallel lines of rope placed horizontally, like railroad tracks, between two other trees.

The tires would be offered to children to roll down the concrete ramp, and the mats would be placed to the side of the ramp so that children could climb up the ramp and jump off it. We would leave the dolly out and see if children wanted to push one another around on it.

By the time people arrived to play, not much was done beyond half of the rope swing hanging limply on one tree. This sad start had taken almost a full hour of effort and finally necessitated a rope-tethered rock being thrown precisely between two high branches, a feat that took many, many tries.

The lack of play apparatus did not seem to matter to those who had come to the event. Mothers appeared with children, blankets, and lunches; they made fires. Tires were rolled down the ramp as anticipated; leaps were made onto mats. Children sat on the dolly and were pushed pell-mell, screaming, by other children. Babies slept.

Eventually, the skeleton of the rope swing emerged, look-

The rope swing being tested at the pop-up playground

ing like a giant pi sign hanging between two trees. All that was needed was a seat for the swing. Noriko suggested one of the half logs; perfect.

I felt like it was only good manners to let the many children who had come to play for the day sit on the swing before I went. And indeed, the line for the swing formed almost immediately and didn't abate until late afternoon.

But at last, not long before we took it down, I had my turn on the swing. The log seat was low to accommodate the small children who were there, and it was even lower with my weight, but still, it held me, and I backed up until I was on my tiptoes, as tall as I could possibly make myself, like a ballerina *en pointe,* and then I picked up my feet and let go.

I flew between the trees. I flew gently, easily, as if it were the most natural thing in the world to fly, as if flying were easy, as if the trees themselves – the generous, benevolent trees – wanted nothing more than to encourage me in this act.

And I was there, flying while sitting on the seat, which was also the tree, knowing that the swing was going to be disassembled momentarily, knowing that the whole thing was going to be over in a minute, as the sun was going down, as the sun was going to be gone, as it was going to get so dark it would be as if the sun had never been there in the first place, and all this knowing-swinging combined to make me feel like I was bobbing around in a tree womb, where what a tree was, and is, is constantly transforming, a type of supernatural plastic, and I, too, could be like this, could be anything and go anywhere from here.

The swing went up and the monkey bridge went up, and, eventually, at the end of the day, everything came down, and everything was returned, Cat in the Hat–like, to the shed, and the park returned to its emptiness, and Noriko pulled her tin whistle out of her backpack, and I and a dozen other new friends followed her, as if she were the Pied Piper, down the road to the restaurant for dinner, singing along as she played the theme song from the movie *My Neighbor Totoro.*

This was the dinner at which several young people slept over their cocktails. I was sober and awake, however, and I heard it clearly when one of the more quiet and serious of my new companions challenged me to eat the two glassy eyes out of the giant raw fish he had ordered for the group.

Monkey bridge, pop-up playground

I thought briefly of the Japanese girls with the headsets at the Shinagawa Aquarium, holding up bits of fish.

I chomped the eyeballs, smiling.

The table burst into applause.

| 8 |

Each night, just as I thought we were about to leave the play-park and go home so I could finally rest, Noriko would re-member: notes. She had to write her notes.

In theory, this was a beautiful thing. Noriko and at least one if not both of her assistants, two young men in their twenties named Taka and Huta, would meet at the playpark hut – the most craptastically decorated space I have ever seen, with the most fabulous sedimentary layers of interesting junk on junk imaginable – and sit at the low table, the young men smoking cigarettes, as they all diligently wrote their notes about the day in longhand. It usually took about an hour. I felt in these quiet moments, sitting with them, that I was in some sort of *Paradise Lost* study hall.

I had asked Noriko what exactly she wrote in these notes and what the purpose of them was, and I learned that the notes were gathered and brought to the bimonthly meetings at the playpark where the day-to-day operations of the park were discussed and that after that, the notes were stored and referred to as needed.

Still, I couldn't really imagine what she was writing. *Ossan stopped by? We made ramen for lunch?*

No, she said, it was not just what happened that she wrote about, but the struggles of the day. And to further illustrate, she translated her writing from that day, an entry in which she was detailing that she had decided that it might be nice to let the children paint the big slide and so she had brought the paint out from the supply hut. But she was torn, she had written. She wanted the slide to be painted brightly so the paint would show clearly and people would be attracted to the playpark, but the children liked to mix all the paint together, so the many bright colors became one color, a brown, and that brown, which they began painting with, didn't really show up on the slide at all.

And as she was struggling, she wrote, with whether to tell the children to stop following their impulses to mix the paint and with her own desire to use bright colors, and with her knowledge that she should not interfere unless it was really necessary, she was simultaneously worrying that her own conflicting feelings about the situation were creating a bad "atmosphere." That was her word. So she backed off and said nothing and let the children paint the slide as they saw fit, meaning brown, and pretty much invisibly, and she painted the picnic tables in bright colors herself, with assistance from me.

I was surprised when she told me this was what she was writing; it seemed impossible that she was truly of two minds over what I thought of as a teeny-tiny intervention and even more impossible that she was going to the trouble to document this uncertainty on paper, in longhand. The whole process seemed so . . . ancient.

And yet, bulldozing a space, padding and disinfecting it, and then congratulating ourselves on how we can sit back with our handhelds and leave our babies and children alone to "explore" is just one approach. It has its drawbacks, however, including the fact that babies and children, who quickly become young adults, do not learn how to take risks in space, something that ultimately makes them less safe in space, not more.

Allowing babies, children, and young adults to spend as much time as possible with the lowest level of interference in the highest-quality environment we can provide for them—that is, an environment that we have not engineered ourselves and do not completely control, an environment we don't fully understand, an environment that includes devils and angels and accidents and trees and swings and lunch—this is another approach. It also has drawbacks, the major ones being the pain of our own uncertainty and vulnerability, the process of making peace with the unknown, and the requirement that a noninterfering adult Be Here Now.

But it would be worth it, if we could do this. Americans, I beseech you, it is not as impossible as it seems. We may have an ocean on the east and west, we may have our borders on the north and south, but we are not an island; we are in the world. There is no escaping it: we have been born, we are going to die.

Americans, I beg you: Recognize! We are already in Savage Park!

5

MORE

| 1 |

When the earthquake and tsunami hit Japan, I thought of Yelena increasingly and was relieved when she e-mailed to say that she had made it to the airport with Chuck, Gen, and the baby and that they were camping out there overnight with the intention of getting on the next flight to New York and staying for a couple of weeks with Yelena's parents, who lived on the Upper West Side.

She e-mailed: *I packed one tiny carry-on for all of us. would you happen to have some spare big-boy clothes we could borrow for three weeks?? . . . we are camping out at the airport tonight and barring any further disasters boarding a plane tomorrow . . . whew . . .*

KOJI TAKIGUCHI

Adults hanging out,
Hanegi Playpark

I e-mailed Noriko too, for the first time since her wedding in December, to say that I was thinking of her, and I learned that she and her new husband were in Nagano, which is in the middle of the country, west of Tokyo. Her baby was due March 12, one day after the earthquake hit. It was March 16 when I heard from her. No labor yet.

Because of the earthquake, the baby is staying in, she wrote.

| 2 |

During my week with Noriko, I had only about three hours when I was entirely on my own. I told her one day when we were at the playpark that I had to go and buy my boys some toys, because I had promised them I would. If I don't bring them toys when I come home, they will kill me, I said.

Noriko looked at me with narrowed eyes. People don't bandy about the word *kill* in her circles.

"Not really," I said apologetically.

She let me go. I was headed to a toy store I had been to with the boys when we were guests of Yelena a year earlier. It was a completely delightful five-floor toy emporium called Kiddyland on a tony Tokyo shopping street, the Omotesando.

I ran from the playpark to the train and promptly got lost. I wandered around the wrong neighborhood asking hipsters to help me get back on track. It was the day before I was going to go home and I was simultaneously so excited about my freedom and so terrified of my freedom that I could barely act; I wanted to do so many things that I didn't know what to do, and after I spent half my time getting lost, I did not have time, in the end, to do anything but what I was supposed to do, which was buy toys for King and Mick, some candy for visitors to the playpark, and a gift for Noriko.

I finally walked through the familiar red doors of Kiddyland and ran to the basement, where I knew the toy vehicles were, and bought trucks and trains for the boys. It took me a while and I was panicking about time when I realized I still needed to get Noriko a gift.

I went back up to the ground floor and looked around; that's where they kept the seasonal items, which, as it was mid-November, were just starting to be Christmas-y. It's also where they displayed the impulse buys, the toys that do the most moving and quacking, similar to what you will see in New York City when you walk past a closet-size "store" that sells T-shirts and see, sitting on the sidewalk, some battery-powered, plastic frogs splashing in a Tupperware container.

I was drawn to a pyramid of moving, plastic toys; they were little, round, friendly, big-headed creatures, solar-powered, with huge, painted-on smiles. They sat and bobbed their heads ecstatically from side to side as the sun shone. They came in many bright colors. I grabbed a neon-green one for Noriko. This would be the equivalent of a visitor to New York City buying her hostess a magnet of the Empire State Building.

We ate breakfast together in her tiny apartment the next morning, having taken the small low, circular table reserved for eating from where we stored it flat against a wall after each meal and on which she placed the most excellent food, hot off what was essentially a camp stove, along with fresh produce she kept in a dorm fridge. I gave her the smiling, plastic, bobbing green thing and watched her, for just a second, look totally horrified before she put her smile back on for me.

And I realized, looking around, that my little green smiling man was probably the only piece of plastic in her entire apartment, which was furnished, with utmost simplicity, with the necessities of life and mementos from friends. Two white T-shirts from play conferences, each signed in black Sharpie by at least twenty people, hung on her wall on simple wire hangers with all the quiet authority of a pair of Cy Twomblys. They were the main décor of her home.

I tried to apologize for my poor choice, but it was too late. The gift was given.

We ate together in silence, enduring each other like sisters.

Savage Park

| 3 |

The latest news report offered a UN group's tracking of the probable course of the radiation plume from Japan: it should hit Southern California by Friday, the paper said.

Japan is here, it seems. Yelena and the boys made it to the city and came over to our place. It was nice, as if she were a neighbor. King and Mick and Chuck and Gen played like old friends, shooting one another with toy guns. I met the new baby, Aevi.

Coincidentally, my friend Bill Burke was in town from Boston and dropped by with his giant black German shepherd, Omar, who is named for the character on the TV show *The Wire*. Bill is a photographer of Vietnam/guns/motorcycles/snakes/weirdoes/himself. His 1987 book *I Want to Take Picture* is well known in photography circles.

He is working on a new series of photos called *Destrukto*. They are very large images of objects being shot with a gun. A can of Yoo-hoo, for instance, set against a black-and-white-tile background, is seen spinning, liquid spewing, at the moment the bullet is shredding it. It's Gilbert and George meet *Apocalypse Now*.

This was more people than I had had in my apartment at once in a long time, and I tried to take pictures myself, but the batteries in my digital camera were running low, and I couldn't see what I was aiming at through the screen of the viewfinder. Despite my restarting the camera repeatedly, it remained black. I kept looking at the screen anyway, out of habit, long after I recognized that the batteries were low, as if this situation were going to change, as if the screen were somehow going to come back to life and help me see what I was shooting at.

I was nearing the point of throwing the camera down in disgust and not even trying to take pictures at all when I thought: *Just let go. Just let the camera take the picture on its own.*

| 4 |

I got an e-mail from Noriko's husband, Haruki, on Monday. Yelena was also cc'd on it. Noriko had her baby, a girl named Nico, on March 21.

Great mother already, Haruki wrote about Noriko.

He put some photos on his Facebook page. Peering at the screen, I saw that Noriko had had a home birth. I could see a signature-strewn T-shirt on a hanger on the wall, as it had been in her old apartment. There were two midwives there, hovering near her in gloves and masks. In one image, Noriko nurses the baby in bed as Haruki kneels, right hand holding the scissors open, about to cut the cord.

| 5 |

March 24, I got another e-mail from Haruki.

Nico died in her sleep after just two days alive; they didn't know why.

They were having a prayer service at 2:00 p.m. and wanted everyone to join them.

I texted Yelena immediately. We were both sick with the news.

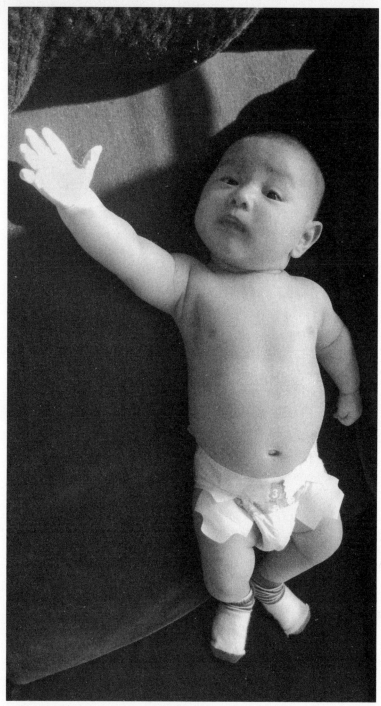

Aevi

When is 2:00 p.m. there? I asked.

Either 1:00 p.m. today or 1:00 a.m. last night, she wrote. But I don't think it matters.

| 6 |

To play, you do not need a particular object or game or even a playground; you need only an assent, a grateful and glad *yes*.

Granting this yes, to and for ourselves, in every environment, even awful ones, is one of the most liberating things humans can do.

I am thinking of this idea this winter. It's still winter, even though it's the end of March. I am still wearing the puffy uniform – down coat, corduroys, hat, boots – that I first donned in November. I think it has adhered to my skin.

I shepherd the boys to school on the subway and then I shepherd them home on the subway, in the cold and snow and wind, twice a day, back and forth, back and forth.

It's like we are moving so much we aren't moving; we are poised here, totally still.

Lately, on the train ride, I let the boys eat Tic-Tacs, which I didn't let them do at the beginning of the school year. I broke down in February. We buy them now at the newsstand at the Forty-Second Street station, where we change trains.

After we buy a box for them to share, they sit on the train and talk about the colors and flavors and the fact that Katie calls Tic-Tacs *tactics*.

As long as I hear their voices and the box shaking like a maraca, I feel free to sit there on the hard, gray seat with them, tip my head back, and close my eyes.

PART II

6

SSOF

Katie is on a roll where she is getting up every day at 5:30 a.m. We have this quiet time together each morning, while the boys and Frank are sleeping.

"Do you know Noriko?" Katie asks me one morning, a few days after Noriko's baby's death.

I carry her to the kitchen to set her on the counter while I start the coffee.

"Yes," I say. I assume she has heard me mention Noriko's name.

"Noriko is sad," she says.

"I know," I say, pouring the coffee grounds into the press.

"Do you know Noriko's baby?" she asks.

"Yes," I say, eyeing her.

"Noriko's baby went into the air," she says.

I put the bag of coffee down to look at her. She is not getting this language from me.

"And then what happened?" I ask her.

She thinks. "And then the baby flew away," she says.

I better follow this as far as I can, I think.

"And then what happened?"

She eats a raisin.

"I don't know," she says finally.

The water boils. I pour it on the grounds.

Reading the news about the power plant in Japan feels like watching a terrifying Rube Goldberg–like contraption unfold in its slow-motion, clunky pattern toward an unthinkable end. I should probably stop watching, but I can't.

Yelena was supposed to come over with the boys again today but Gen is sick and she decided to stay put at her mom's. I am waiting to see if there is another time we can get together before her flight back to Tokyo. When I saw her last, she told me her mom had begged her to leave the three grandkids with her on the Upper West Side. She was trying to convince Yelena that Yelena should go back to Japan—she has a teaching job at a university there—without them.

I said I understood her mom's point; I don't know if I would take three young kids to Tokyo right now.

But I also understood Yelena's point; oh yes, I did. She wanted to be with her kids in her own space.

| 2 |

A year and a half after I visited her, Noriko came to New York. She stopped here and stayed with us for a couple of days as part of a longer jaunt across the United States. She had never been to New York before.

It was spring when she came, and the weather was just starting to turn. The boys were still in school. Noriko and I spent most of her time here walking around. She wanted to see Ground Zero, so that was one of the first places we went.

I stood with her at the viewing area in the World Financial Center. A busload of American tourists had just arrived and were swarming around us, asking one another loudly where the Starbucks was.

Noriko stood so close to the bank of floor-to-ceiling windows that her nose was touching the glass. She stood there silently. I saw that her face was wet with tears.

I stepped back to give her privacy. The bus riders were like ions pinging around us, shouting out random names of coffee drinks.

Finally, after ten minutes, Noriko mopped her face with her bandanna, shoved her bandanna back in her pocket, and turned to me.

"Shall we go?" I asked softly.

We walked along the path by the Hudson River slowly, like old women, stopping to admire the buds on the trees.

| 3 |

It's been a week since Noriko's baby died. I e-mailed her three times over the last five days, which I know may be too frequently, but I can't stop myself.

I am thinking of you, I am so sorry, I hope you are doing all right. I write these words.

Days pass.

| 4 |

Mick is playing a new game on the walk home from the subway station. He is very aware of movement and symmetry — he is wired like a dancer, I think, though he wants to be in the NFL — and it does not surprise me when he explains that the idea of the game is that as you walk along the right side of the sidewalk in one direction, you must be aware of the person who is coming toward you on your left; when the person is at the point where he is directly beside you, you have to make sure that your foot does not touch the ground at the same time his does; you cannot mirror his step. You ensure this by jumping.

When you walk down the street with Mick, then, on the way home from school, you watch him watch the approach of other people very carefully, and then when someone is beside him, you watch him leap, seemingly ecstatically, into the air. In fact, he is not ecstatic; he is trying not to die. Because the idea in this game is that if you step along the same line that the other person is stepping on – if you mirror him in his step – you will die. So when that person is directly beside you, moving in the opposite direction, you must make sure you are in the air.

This game – which looks like Mick leaping happily and randomly down the fairly industrial block our home is on – is called, naturally, war.

I don't think Mick has explained the rules of this game to King even though King is always with us when we do this walk. This is fine, because King is busy with his own game. We get to the spot on our block just past the security camera – I wouldn't even have seen the security camera perched like a gargoyle above the office-building entrance if King hadn't pointed it out – and once we are just past it, he asks me to "release" him, which means count backward from five and say "Blastoff!," because the moment he passes the security camera's gaze, he transforms into a long-range cruise missile, and – after blastoff – he runs all the way home, so far ahead of Mick and me that I have to hop up and down to make sure I still see his blue hat bobbing along the sidewalk, since Mick, who is very busy in his leaping/defying-death alongside strangers, cannot be rushed.

| 5 |

Today Katie spends a full minute jumping on her trampoline exclaiming in a grief-stricken voice, "I had a baby! Now I have nothing!"

| 6 |

In the time since Mick, King, Frank, and I first visited Yelena in Tokyo – it's been five years now – I wouldn't say I have done a spectacular job of providing any particularly Hanegi Playpark–ian experience for my boys here in New York. The boys are seven and nine now, and they hammer and do home repair occasionally with Frank. We grow flowers and vegetables on our terrace amid the truck exhaust. I let them jump on the couch cushions. They play the piano more or less reluctantly. That's about it.

What I have done, I hope, is try to keep this idea of Play Freely at Your Own Risk in mind as much as possible and try to communicate to the boys that playing is not what we are here for, necessarily, or even what we are doing here, but how we are here.

I don't know if I am having much success. King has started homework this year and despite my theories, play, for him, is not a state of consciousness. It is not really an action either, though. It is more a way of saying "freedom."

When King says he wants to play before doing his homework, what he means is that he wants the time/space to not be bothered by me. What he does in that time/space is not that important – he likes to read, draw, build, play ball, and chat with Mick. Whatever he chooses, the critical part is that he is not directed.

He is keen to seek this unfetteredness, and his viewpoint humbles me. For all my fussing about playground aesthetics, he does not really care too much about the kind of playground he is in. If the space is padded and disinfected, fine. If it's Savage Park, fine. The environment is not the issue. The issue is the degree to which he perceives that he is free, and for the most part, *free* means being left alone to do what he wants.

Of course, what he wants is not always possible – no, you can't punt the football in the living room – and this has made me think about his freedom, or relative lack of it, and try to think of what we can do to feel more free.

It's amazing to discover how difficult this is. It's ridiculous, and the boys know it, but I have taken to calling blank sheets of paper SSOFs, or Sacred Squares of Freedom. The name came about because King had a homework assignment about the political turmoil in Egypt, and Mick was reading over King's shoulder. Later that night I asked Mick what we should suggest as the name of his Little League baseball team, and he said, "Protesting People of Egypt."

"Nice," I said. "PPOE."

His team is called the Neptunes.

King's having homework has been a hard transition for Mick, who misses being able to play with his brother after school. Frequently, when King starts his homework, Mick tries to undermine him by standing next to him and flying paper airplanes in his face or the like.

To prevent this, I have been sitting Mick down at the SSOFs while King works. Draw whatever you want, I say. Write whatever you want.

So far, most of the images Mick has drawn have been astronauts. And one word: *poop.*

| 7 |

It is hard to watch the Japanese struggle with their damaged nuclear reactor in what seems like such an inept way. I keep thinking this is the flipside of a culture that can create, and tolerate, the fragile/brilliant mess of Savage Park.

I say to Frank one night: Americans would have been on that reactor like white on rice.

| 8 |

I have mom-friends who tell me how wrong I am about various screen-based activities for kids, how great these things are, and how creative – they use that word – their children have been in, for instance, making a really cute birthday card for Grandpa with a particular program online.

I don't know what to say to this in polite conversation, because when I hear things like this about creativity, I want to cry. I want to cry because my understanding of creativity is that creativity, in its fullest, most cherry-blossom-ish flowering, wants to piss on your grave.

Creativity is like this because it is a force; it is powerful, overwhelming, fiery, and insatiable, and it cannot and should not be satisfied with arranging virtual flowers on a two-dimensional template that was structured by a greeting-card-company employee who was thinking about God knows what. Creativity wants to set fire to every greeting card you ever made. Creativity wants Grandpa to die already so it can race his Oldsmobile off the dock and into the lake.

Creativity is like this because creativity is part destroyer, and in my limited experience, this is why real creativity does not get many party invitations.

But this is the good thing about creativity, too: it is a party crasher. So if there is just a little, tiny space – an opening – that is enough, thank you, for creativity to find its way through.

| **9** |

The last night I was in the playpark, after Bailey's Milk played; after Noriko and I had been sitting around with teenagers in the evening; after the teenagers played their songs on guitar and sang and smoked; after a young man who came to practice his moves twirled a giant, fiery baton; after we all went out to eat noodles together; after we went back to the playpark after the restaurant to get Noriko's backpack because we'd forgotten it; after all that, we discovered that there was a serious discussion going on between one of the women who was on the playpark committee and Taka and Huta, Noriko's play-worker assistants.

My heart sank when we encountered this. Everything takes a long time in Japan, but serious conversations take even longer. *We will never get home,* I thought.

Noriko was pretending to look for something on a shelf but I saw that she was listening intently. I glared at her.

I. want. to. go, I said with my eyebeams.

She ignored me.

I heard the playpark woman saying "Mmm, mmm" to Taka. It was like hearing a mother coo to a baby underwater. An interpersonal situation was being smoothed over.

I sat down near the door and closed my eyes, resigned.

Noriko walked over and ushered me out of the hut. We stood on the porch.

"I have to stay," she whispered, "but I have my key."

She dangled it in front of me, looking straight in my eyes.

"Do you know the way home?" she asked.

"Yes," I lied.

She gave the key to me, then turned around and padded back into the warm light of the hut.

I turned and walked in the opposite direction, into the dark of the playpark. It was midnight. I was alone.

I took a deep breath and smelled the playpark smell, which, in November, is the smell of leaves and dirt and water and noodles and smoke. It's a fantastic smell, earthy and fresh.

I walked to where I had first stood with King when the Japanese gentleman had offered us marshmallows on sticks. I looked up at the trees in the dark.

Then I walked out of the park. I walked past the gaggle of unlocked bicycles, past the concrete, S-shaped-ravine playground, past the baseball field, past the traditional playground where we had come that very first time with Yelena and her family, and then out of Hanegi Koen altogether and into the street.

I realized how much time I had spent on this walk not paying attention to where I was going, following Noriko blindly, chatting, as she walked her bike alongside me.

I took the key in my right hand and held it in front of me, at arm's length, like a divining rod.

As I kept walking I decided to flip the key so I was holding it with the teeth up. The key became a shark at the end of my hand, a shark that was using sonar, a shark that did not need to see well to swim, a shark that was going to smell its way to the one lock in the one door in the one apartment in the one building in this big city that its teeth just perfectly fit in.

It was a Sunday night. The streets were completely deserted. There was absolutely no sound. Tokyo was like the stage set for a city, and all the cast members had gone home.

I did not have a cell phone. I did not have the language to use a cell phone. I did not even know, in words, Noriko's address.

I had never been as completely alone and lost as I was in that moment. I was hyperventilating. I tried to slow my breathing.

I focused on my shark. My shark wanted to go up higher so he could smell better. I held him up there, over my head.

I stopped thinking as much as I possibly could. I switched my center of operations from my brain to my gut. I listened to my shark with my gut. My gut and the shark were a team. If you drew a curved line between my shark and my gut, there was a fin of awareness between them.

The awareness became thick, like smoke, then clear and sparkly; finally, it transformed into a sail.

I was blown along in the dark, down the silent streets, past the small, papery houses, under the giant moon and stars. I couldn't feel my body moving, though I heard my breathing. I was gliding.

Finally I saw the steps of Noriko's building. I lowered my shark and found my feet and started to think.

I bounded up the steps gratefully, with humility, moved

by the miracle that the streets of Tokyo had taken care of me, had spoken to me without language, without sound, with only vibration, as I put the key in the lock that fit beautifully and twisted my wrist and opened the door.

I felt the slow twirl of the world as I pulled off my boots and sat down at Noriko's old computer and typed an incoherent love note to Frank in the e-mail text box and then sent it, with the watery wave of one finger, to the other side of the globe.

7

RED BUTTERFLIES

| 1 |

When Noriko came to visit us in New York, which was between the time when I visited her and the time she met and married Haruki, I had a party for her. It was nowhere near as fabulous as Bailey's Milk playing in the playpark, but I invited a bunch of friends over, people I hoped Noriko would like, and we sat around and talked and everyone ate barbecue.

Noriko was still very open about her desire to have a child, even though she hadn't met her future husband yet and was not even entirely confident that that would ever happen.

Noriko received a small beaded box as a gift from one of my friends. Someone joked to her that her future baby was in there.

I watched as Noriko clutched the tiny empty box to her chest and hugged it delightedly.

| 2 |

I wonder if it would be possible, in our country, for great hordes of people to go to a place like Savage Park with the same ease with which we go to, say, a chain restaurant for dinner, only instead of anticipating an atmosphere that is clean, warm, and nice, instead of anticipating an engagement with the mommy in space that will present us with yummy cheddar fries and Diet Cokes and then make the dirty dishes disappear, a mommy-sphere that will keep us, in some ways, infantilized, we would anticipate a connection with a different mommy in space who is not entirely known, who is mysterious and powerful, who gets grumpy and demands respect.

Could we, as a people, as a culture, be willing to easily and regularly face the mommy in our environment who enables our existence? Who can take it away?

If not in a playground, where?

If not now, when? At the moment of death? That one time? That's it?

| 3 |

When I was in my twenties, before I had children, I met Ettore Sottsass Jr., the legendary architect and designer who was the founder of the Memphis design group. Sottsass, who was born in Vienna but went to school and practiced in Italy, designed everything from homes to airports to ceramic vases to, in 1969, the iconic bright red Olivetti Valentine portable typewriter, which was the Apple of its generation.

Sottsass died on December 31, 2007, at the age of ninety.

In my twenties, I worked at an art magazine, and I went to Milan to interview him. I had never been there before. I looked out the airplane window at the Alps as we flew over them. I was shocked at their majesty. Then I went back to fitful sleep in the overly formal outfit I had chosen to wear for the plane ride.

In addition to all his design and architecture work, Sottsass published several books of his photographs. One, *The Curious Mr. Sottsass: Photographing Design and Desire,* contains a brief passage he wrote called "War." Sottsass registered for the Italian army in World War II and spent most of the war in a Yugoslavian concentration camp.

"There was nothing courageous or enjoyable about the ridiculous war I fought in. I learned nothing from it. It was a complete waste of time," it begins.

Sottsass was ill when I arrived; I was supposed to have the interview on my first day in Milan but his assistant told me no, I would have to wait until the last day of my trip, three days later, if I were even able to interview him at all.

I was slightly hysterical about not being able to accomplish what I came for, but what could I do? I spent my time wandering around nervously, eating gelato.

Finally, my last day there, I got the call. He could see me.

As quickly as possible, I took a cab from my hotel to his

apartment, which was in a graceful marble building down-town.

I buzzed and was let in. His apartment was on the fifth floor. I pushed the button for the elevator but the elevator did not come.

I couldn't wait.

I waited.

I couldn't wait.

I ran up the steps, the five flights of white marble, with my heart flying. The thing I loved so much about Sottsass, aside from the fact that he made beautiful objects, was that he saw that the entire process of building and making was, in many ways, absurd. He made ceramics in part because they were humble and fragile. He made giant, wildly colored, seven-foot ceramic vases that cost thousands of dollars. He made a small ceramic flower vase in the shape of a pale pink penis – the Shiva vase – and, in marketing it, pasted an image of the vase onto a newspaper photo of two Italian heads of government having a meal. He was a punk of the highest order.

He went through a whole period where he renounced ar-chitecture and design and wandered around the Italian coun-tryside, camping and making structures out of sticks and string, which he photographed.

He photographed constantly. He photographed doors he never opened. He photographed beds where he had just had sex. He was not a decorator and yet he was just a decorator. He had great tenderness for the ways in which people tried to make their lives more comfortable, more bearable, more beautiful.

I don't know what he must have thought of me, some sweaty American girl bounding up the steps to his landing, near tears. He welcomed me into his modest, elegant home.

"What have you been doing today?" I asked him breathlessly, my first interview question. I had just hit the door. I wasn't even holding a pen yet.

He showed me, shyly, where he had been sitting in the dark, on the couch, watching videos of Billie Holiday. He had been drawing pictures of her mouth. He showed me the pages of his sketchbook: bright red butterflies, fluttering their wings.

| 4 |

When you first have a baby, after the labor, and the staying at the hospital for a couple days, and the baby in and out of the nursery getting tested, and the doctor visiting you, and the nurse checking in on you, and the monitoring and more monitoring, finally, after all that, God willing, they say okay and let you and the baby go.

And the doctors and the nursing staff don't say this, but it is there: You are on your own now. The baby is yours. Just don't kill it.

Frank and I laughed when we said this to each other: Just don't kill the baby! And it was such a relief to laugh because of course, the baby, in so many ways, is so terrifying, and your burden, so small, eight pounds, is so gigantic. You bring this small bundle home, you are responsible for it, and it is so fragile, and you don't know what you are doing, and you want so much for it, you have so many hopes, and now, also, you are totally screwed, because the baby may die, your baby may die in a thousand million ways, so many ways you can't even think of them all.

And now this is on you, the parent, to be vigilant and awake and alert and aware every second – yes, to Be Here Now every single second – to protect the baby from dying and to counterattack that harsh reality we made up as a joke: that the only way the baby would die is if we killed him, ha!

And really, this is where there should be some moment in the hospital, some moment where you, as a new parent, take an oath. There should be a moment where you raise your right hand and repeat after the nurse: "First, do no harm," even though that particular phrase was not actually written to apply to newborn babies and is not in fact part of the Hippocratic oath at all, as is widely assumed; it's a paraphrase of a line that comes from the wider body of writings associated with Hippocrates. "First, do no harm" is meant to underscore the two ideas that, like the twin serpents on the caduceus staff, every medical intervention, no matter how well-meaning, carries risks, and that sometimes some people are broken in such a way that they cannot be helped.

Yet in this respect, "First, do no harm" would be a good thing for new parents to say if they also understood it as a double-edged reminder. The oath would mean: Above all, do not hurt the child, of course. But also, do not deny the possibility that your child may be hurt beyond your ability to make her better, and, finally, do not do the opposite of denying the possibility, which is becoming obsessed with it. There has to be some middle ground.

| 5 |

Mick is very into music now and he has been playing a lot of music and as a result we have been doing a lot of dancing in our apartment lately. Everyone has his or her style. King has a lot of breakdancing and ninja moves. Katie does the toddler Frankenstein. Mick is more fluid. When he is really in a groove, he stands on top of the kid-size table and assumes a jogging posture, and then he moves really slowly, as if he were slow-motion speed skating. He inevitably does this to a really bright, fast song, and when he does it, he is always half smiling. It is a secret he is in on: the music that envelops us is fast and light, but the world each of us is in, the body, is slow and plodding.

| 6 |

American playgrounds that are designed to adhere to the regulations of the Consumer Product Safety Commission and that are subject to reviews by certified playground inspectors and that have instructions for uniform installment of playground equipment that are specific down to the half inch – these kinds of structures are fantasies for adults, fantastic fortress images we build to reassure ourselves that death will not happen to our children there. They are temples to that idea.

The idea that we – and our children – are never really "safe" is hard to live with. But the good news is that we also don't have to live with the opposite idea–that we are always "unsafe."

Moving beyond the dichotomy of safe/unsafe, beyond I won't die/I am dying, where are we? For most of us, most of the time, we are in a place where we are neither totally "safe" nor "unsafe." We are in time, in space, we are living.

| 7 |

At the time of Sottsass's death, he was the subject of a retrospective exhibition at a gallery in Trieste. His work was laid out on seven tables. You sailed around the gallery and visited the table islands, and while you were examining it all, you listened on a headset to him talking about the objects and buildings and his process.

So many architects – architects in particular! – at the ends of their lives become invested in staging monolithic shows about the importance of their buildings/themselves, but here, Sottsass had put together an exhibition with the grace and humility of a yard sale and had made his own little mix tape for it.

It was not a show about having all the answers. The title of it was *I Want to Know Why*.

8

AMERICAN WIND

| 1 |

In being married to Frank, who is a flea-market and thrift-store devotee, I have had the opportunity to observe someone, over time, whose habits regarding objects are very different from my own. We actually have opposing perspectives on objects, which makes for an interesting household.

If we were to play a game called "how we deal with objects," and if this game were played by the rules of my childhood game of war, the two sides could be broken down as follows: Frank's side believes that all objects are a type of pet, and for owners like Frank, this is part of their charm. Objects are part of their owner's family. They never leave their adopted home voluntarily; when they do leave, it is always due to a sad or unfortunate circumstance that forced their departure. The acquiring of an object is a joyful event.

My side also believes that objects are a type of pet, but for owners like me, instead of being a comfort or a charm, this quality is a burden. The fewer objects owned, the better.

Frank and I are not quite at war over this. We play at getting and then getting rid of things. And I appreciate a fantastic object as much as the next guy. Maybe even more, because I believe that making an object is a greater task, really, than making a human.

Getting pregnant is not always easy, but making a human, once you are pregnant, *is* easy. You are not the architect; you are the clay. The architect works through you. You have no choice; you yourself are the object. You are sculpted.

In being human and making an object, you are also sculpted, but the process is much more subtle. You yourself are sculpted by your actions. It is a much slower and more delicate process than gestating, which is pretty dramatic in comparison.

In making an object and being finely sculpted by that process, you have the whole world to choose from in terms of your medium, and every one of your choices, good or bad, is reflected in you, on and in your body.

Objects are greater miracles than people, then, because we humans have no fantastic-genius architect working through us when we want to build a toilet: We have to figure everything out. We have to make it all up, and we don't know everything.

Maybe this is the great development of the technological age: People make objects now like it's nothing. It's not magic anymore. It's not even important. Objects – amazing objects – are everywhere. We are drowning in them.

We make all this stuff, and yet, I am convinced, we don't know what any of it is. We don't see how objects live; we don't recognize the glacial pace of their aging process. We don't see that we look like blurs to them; we don't recognize how we are like rainbow lights zooming by until we stop and touch them. At those moments, we come into focus for them like ghostly forms on infrared cameras. *There she is,* the sugar bowl thinks: *Mommy.*

They sometimes threw objects in black plastic bags and sent them away on boats to be buried, our children's children will say, shaking their heads.

| 2 |

Women who have been through childbirth have a leg up on dying, I think. They have been at least partway to that place, that life/death place, and they know some of what it means to be in pain and vulnerable there.

I recently heard a talk about assisting the dying, and there was a lot of talk about dying "with dignity," and I have to say, I wasn't sure what that meant at first. A lot of the same emotions and events that often present themselves in childbirth – pain, loss of bowel control, anger, withdrawal – are associated with dying. Some women say they are nervous about pooping on the delivery table, but in my experience, a doctor or nurse waves a hand and says it's perfectly normal and not to worry, no one cares. No one talks about dignity, although that is exactly what the mom-to-be is concerned about. It is scary to think about being so incredibly undignified, sweating and grunting and pooping, in pain, in front of other people. It *is* undignified, though, it just is, and it can't be made dignified because you have to stay present. You can't just be knocked out, because you have to think about the baby.

In death, there is no baby; you are birthing yourself. Dying with dignity, I think, means that you are not alone in that birth experience, and you are not screaming in pain. You are clean and calm and appropriately medicated and, ideally, with a loved one.

I don't know what the hardest thing about death is; I don't know how hard it is to die. Maybe for a person who is dying with dignity, death itself is not so bad. Maybe it can be a good birth.

| 3 |

For myself, I believe that no matter the circumstances of death, after death, there is a place you go to, or maybe go back to.

There is a reality twin.

| 4 |

Often, my boys want to play war games. They want to pretend they are in battle; they want to throw sticks and rocks; they want to read books about modern fighting helicopters; they want to amass Pokémon armies; they want to play hair-raising computer games where they are transformed into tanks that drive around and shoot at other tanks.

They have always loved Legos, but this winter they began a new building project that was more ambitious than any Frank and I had previously seen.

It started with a spinning top someone gave Mick for his birthday. It was a really nice top, metal; a modern take on the world's oldest toy. A Beyblade, it was called. I hadn't seen a spinning top like that since Japan; the kids I saw there played with wooden ones they call *beigoma*.

Mick has acquired a million Lego sets and in the process has amassed some really odd-looking pieces, including several dome-shaped ones, each about the size of a dime. Mick discovered that when he affixed a dome-shaped piece to the bottom of any structure, he could spin it. He got the idea to make a spinning top out of Legos.

King got involved. The boys began spending hours in their bedroom making, perfecting, and then naming spinning tops, until at last the tops emerged from the bedroom into the world of the larger apartment for their life purpose: to do battle.

The boys cleared off the now beat-up train table to make an arena. Each boy chose a top he had made, then the two boys did a countdown backward from three and began spinning the tops toward each other on "one."

We all watched the collisions; whichever top survived the clash more intact was the winner.

The tops were breathtaking, with fantastic names: Whirlwind Ravener, Knife Hurricane, Civil War.

I began photographing them, but I am not a patient photographer. Frank got involved. He set the tops on nice paper, positioned them in good light, and photographed them

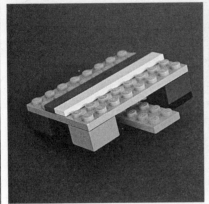

Rockslide Megafortress

Eye of the Sun

Police Brutality

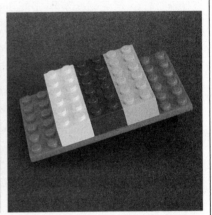

American Wind

Planet

Knife Hurricane

with our most powerful and obedient camera. Whenever a new top materialized, Frank and I would sit there and admire it, proud grandparents.

"Look at that beast," Frank would say with pleasure about a delicately wobbling plastic rectangle.

I watched my sons work with the structure, care, and feeding of these snarling, whirling demons. I was awestruck. Here we all were, in an apartment in the shadow of Times Square, cut off from any grass, in a box with all the windows closed, in winter, with forced heat, and yet, in these plastic pieces, the spiraling power that is life came in and was fighting for recognition, for reverence – here, on our old train table.

It was not real life, of course, in that Red-and-Black Catastrophe whirling was not a real catastrophe; it was art. But that's what is fantastic about art. It is tricky, alive and not, a balancing act.

| 5 |

We are trying to move closer to the boys' schools so we don't have to do this back-and-forth on the train all the time anymore, so we can all walk to school together.

Moving is a huge job; I am depressed. I have been looking at spaces for months. Everything is so small and costs so much. Walls are painted gold to show you that they are valuable. Homes are like walk-in safes. I want to see a home that has not been decorated with the underlying idea of placing expensive objects like stars in a constellation that is ever fixed and means something supposedly really important. I want to see a home that is not, itself, dead. I want to see a home that acknowledges life and death.

This week I went to another apartment appointment. I have long ago stopped looking at apartments with my broker because I can't be bothered to call him up all the time. The apartment is being sold as is, the seller's broker, whom I meet there, says. I am not sure what that means until we get upstairs and I see the place is an empty wreck.

"Why is it like this?" I ask.

He explains that it is a rent-stabilized apartment, which in New York City means that the people who live there usually do not move out until they die. The old tenant who had been there for years finally moved out, he says.

Suddenly, he says, "I remember you. You've been to this building before. You saw the apartment across the hall, the mirror apartment."

We go over the details; he is right. I was here nine months ago and I forgot about it.

I'm ready to move this time, I tell him.

9

THE STRUCTURES
TREMBLE

| 1 |

We have a piece designed by Sottsass. It's from 1979, and it's called *The Structures Tremble*. It's a table that's forty-five inches high with a twenty-inch-square glass top. It's not really good for anything except holding a single object, an object you want to display and adore.

The table itself consists of a square, white laminate base upon which four machinery-like silver cylinders sit. From each silver cylinder, an enameled metal leg, each in a different Easter-egg color – pale blue, yellow, pink, and green – oscillates up and outward, "trembling."

The net effect is of a box upon which someone has placed

The Structures Tremble, *Ettore Sottsass, 1979*

four cheerfully exploding batteries, and on top of the explosion, your object magically floats.

You could put a dirty diaper on that table and it would look fantastic, like it had blown in from the sea and was standing there on a half shell, surrounded by cherubs and combing its luxurious long hair. Everything about an object is more interesting when it is placed on that table; you believe it is something miraculous, something to be worshipped.

Whether the idea behind the design of the table was tongue-in-cheek or not is hard to say. It's a table that is simultaneously terrified and defiant. It is a table that is doing its table work as it naughtily mimics or honestly quakes in fear of the earthquake that, in one fell swoop, will one day destroy every single glass-topped table that now stands.

| 2 |

All objects are broken, because they need us.

All people are broken, in their need for one another.

We are all trembling, people and objects, for one another, all the time.

| 3 |

I wipe Katie's bottom. She has had a fever the last couple of days, and has diarrhea.

She is on her back, looking up at me, poop everywhere.

I love you, she says.

| 4 |

What makes us savage or not is not the tools we pick up and hold in our hands.

What makes us savage or not is not the astonishing objects we devise, and clutch, and look into, and stroke, as if we were at long last finding ourselves there, like Narcissus gazing at the lake.

What makes us savage or not is whether we have the ability to love one another, and have compassion for one another, in light of the fact that we are broken.

What makes us savage or not is the recognition that a girl who comes into the world and stays for less than two days is human; that what joyfully fucked to conceive her was human; that what labored to help her arrive was human; that what prepared her body for cremation was human; that what grieved immeasurably was human and cannot be thrown away.

| 5 |

I can't believe you are moving, Yelena e-mails me when I tell her the news. *Your apartment seems so much a part of you.*

I haven't yet seen the new apartment Yelena lives in, the home she moved into after she divorced R. I do know it's near Hanegi Playpark. They can smell the playpark smoke from her house, she told me.

I asked her how the playground was faring after the earthquake.

The Savage Park rocks, she wrote. *We are there almost every weekend.*

RESOURCES

| SOURCES |

Caillois, Roger. *Man, Play, and Games.* Translated by Meyer
Barash. Urbana: University of Illinois Press, 2001.

Caldwell, Lesley, ed. *The Elusive Child.* London: H. Karnac
Books Ltd., 2002.

Chudacoff, Howard P. *Children at Play: An American History.*
New York: New York University Press, 2007.

Cranz, Galen. *The Politics of Park Design: A History of
Urban Parks in America.* Cambridge, MA: MIT Press,
1982.

Crawford, Chris. *The Art of Computer Game Design:
Reflections of a Master Game Designer.* New York:
McGraw-Hill, 1984.

Dattner, Richard. *Design for Play*. New York: Van Nostrand–Reinhold, 1969.

Farrell, Michael P. *Collaborative Circles: Friendship Dynamics and Creative Work*. Chicago and London: University of Chicago Press, 2001.

Hewes, Jeremy Joan. *Build Your Own Playground! A Sourcebook of Play Sculptures, Designs, and Concepts from the Work of Jay Beckwith*. Boston: Houghton Mifflin, 1975.

Huizinga, Johan. *Homo Ludens: A Study of the Play Element in Culture*. Boston: Beacon Press, 1950.

Ruskin, John. *On Art and Life*. 1853–1859. New York: Penguin Books, 2005.

Salen, Katie, and Eric Zimmerman. *Rules of Play: Game Design Fundamentals*. Cambridge, MA: MIT Press, 2004.

Solomon, Susan. *American Playgrounds: Revitalizing Community Space*. Lebanon, NH: University Press of New England, 2005.

Sutton-Smith, Brian. *The Ambiguity of Play*. Cambridge, MA: Harvard University Press, 1997.

Winnicott, D. W. *Playing and Reality*. New York: Routledge, 1971.

| SOME PLAY RESOURCES OF NOTE |

International Play Association: http://ipaworld.org;
http://ipausa.org

Playpark Setagaya: NPO organization overseeing the
adventure playparks in Tokyo; www.playpark.jp/info
_pp/setagaya.html (in Japanese)

Berkeley Adventure Playground: www.ci.berkeley.ca.us
/adventureplayground/

Imagination Playground: www.imaginationplay
ground.com

Wayfinder Experience: www.wayfinderexperience.com

American Academy of Pediatrics, release on the need
for free play, http://pediatrics.aappublications.org/
content/119/1/182.full.pdf

Alliance for Childhood: www.allianceforchildhood.org

Pop-Up Adventure playgrounds: http://popupadven
tureplaygrounds.wordpress.com

Adventure Playgrounds: http://adventureplaygrounds
.hampshire.edu/history.html

Cas Holman: www.casholman.com

Toni Pizza: www.tonithepizza.com

ScienceDaily, on the importance of free play: www
.sciencedaily.com/releases/2009/04/090415102211
.htm

Ithaca Children's Garden: http://ithacachildrensgarden
.org

Kaboom: Play Matters! http://kaboom.org

ACKNOWLEDGMENTS

Thank you:

To Yelena, Chuck, Gen, and Aevi; to Noriko, Haruki, and their new baby girl, Iraho; to R; to Philippe Petit and Kathy O'Donnell; to Bill Burke; to Hitoshi Shimamura; to Ossan; to Dr. Harry Engel; to Cas Holman; to Marc Hacker; to Koji Takiguchi; to Kevin Hatt; to Sottsass Associati; to Andrew Decker; to Gene Nakazato and Yurie Takeuchi.

To my agent, Susanna Einstein, for finding the right hands for this manuscript; to my editor at Houghton Mifflin Harcourt, Lauren Wein, for a wonderful publishing experience; to Nina Barnett at Houghton Mifflin Harcourt for her help in coordinating every last little thing; to Tracy Roe, whose copyediting greatly improved this manuscript; to Patrick Barry for the beautiful cover design.

To my dear friend Kathy Giuffre for her ongoing support and encouragement of this project.

To my family.